Trolling Big-Water Walleyes

Trolling Big-Water Walleyes

Secrets of the Great Lakes Fishing Guides, Charter Captains, and Walleye Pros

W. H. "Chip" Gross

Black Squirrel Books™

an imprint of The Kent State University Press

Kent, Ohio 44242 www.KentStateUniversityPress.com

BLACK SQUIRREL BOOKS™ ™
Frisky, industrious black squirrels are a familiar sight on the Kent State University campus and the inspiration for Black Squirrel Books™, a trade imprint of The Kent State University Press.
www.KentStateUniversityPress.com

ISBN 978-1-60635-164-2
Manufactured in China

Every effort has been made to obtain permission from individuals whose likenesses appear in photographs and from persons interviewed by the author who are quoted in this book.

Cataloging information for this title is available at the Library of Congress.

17 16 15 14 13 5 4 3 2 1

I've had the same fishing buddy for more than fifty years: Dave Hoy. Pictured on the cover of this book, he's the one without gills. May we have many more years on the water together, Brother. Now, if you could just learn how to properly net a walleye. . . .

Contents

Chapter 1

Why Walleyes?

They don't have the fighting abilities of bass, nor do they possess the aerial acrobatics of trout. They're not even a particularly attractive fish, colored mainly a muted, brownish, yellow-gold. So what is the attraction of walleyes to anglers? Why do sport fishermen across North America spend millions of hours and millions of dollars annually pursuing this overgrown member of the freshwater perch family? In a word: elusiveness.

Walleyes are finicky, will-o-the-wisp fish, often here today and gone tomorrow. In the Great Lakes; sprawling Western reservoirs; and large, North American rivers, they follow schools of baitfish like hungry wolf packs. As the bait moves, they move. How this often translates for anglers is spectacular fishing one day and scarcely a bite or possibly none at all the next.

Similarly, a cold-weather front may move in and completely turn off a walleye's desire to feed. One of the most frustrating times you'll ever experience as a walleye fisherman is seeing your boat's sonar screen filled top to bottom with inverted "hooks"—sonar echoes of fish you strongly suspect are walleyes—but being unable to get the fish to bite no matter what techniques you try.

Yet that's what makes catching walleyes so rewarding when you do succeed. When the complex puzzle that lets you piece together a limit catch is finally solved, the feeling can be euphoric and last for days. But during those days of mentally patting yourself on the back, don't be lulled into thinking the fishing will be the same the next time you're on the water—as it likely won't. Every day on the water is different, and even though you may go to the exact same location and do the exact same things you did the time before, the fish may or may not still be there. And even if they are, they may not bite. Like I said, elusiveness. . . .

Professional walleye tournament angler Mark Martin of Twin Lake, Michigan, likely described walleyes and walleye fishing best. "Catching

The largest member of the freshwater perch family, walleyes are will-o-the-wisp game fish with bipolar personalities; sometimes they bite and sometimes they don't. And to add to an angler's frustration, walleyes can be here today and gone tomorrow as they follow schools of baitfish across miles of open water on the Great Lakes.

walleyes isn't a slam dunk," he said. "In fact, far from it. They're subsurface feeders that don't fight worth a lick and are prone to bipolar mood swings. Because of that, walleyes—in my opinion—are the most challenging of fish."

There's a second reason fishermen pursue walleyes: the fish are excellent table fare. There is no better-tasting fish that swims, freshwater or saltwater. The mild, flaky, succulent white meat of a walleye filet is excellent fried, baked, or broiled, and I've included a favorite recipe of mine for you to try at the end of this book. In the meantime, we'll concentrate on how to catch this elusive species, my favorite game fish.

Why Troll for Walleyes?

Trolling is placing a fishing line into the water with a lure or bait attached and allowing the slow, forward progress of a boat to impart movement to the lure or bait, in turn attracting fish. But why attempt to catch walleyes by trolling? Why not jig, rig, cast, or use any number of other techniques? There are many ways to catch walleyes, but on big water, trolling puts more walleyes in the boat per hour of fishing than any other technique, hands down. Statistically, no other fishing strategy even comes close. When there are untold miles of water to cover in search of walleyes—such as on the Great Lakes—trolling should be your number one, go-to technique. It just makes sense.

I've spent years trolling for walleyes, and all the advice offered in this book is hard won—you can count on it. I'll tell you honestly what works and what doesn't, at least from my experience. But I can't take credit for all the solid information contained in the following pages, not even a large part of it. Through the years, I've had the privilege of fishing with many fishing guides, charter captains, walleyes pros, and other just plain excellent fishermen who have been more than willing to share their walleye-catching secrets. Many of their special insider tips and techniques are included in this book. Thanks, guys, I owe you a trip.

Now, let's get ready to go fishing. . . .

World of the Walleye: A Thumbnail Life History

The largest of nearly 250 species in the family Percidae (perch and darters) in North America, the walleye is also known as pickerel, yellow pike, walleyed pike, and white salmon, among other local names. This toothy predator prefers the clear to slightly turbid waters of large

A walleye's eyes are well adapted to feeding in low-light conditions, often resulting in dawn, dusk, or even the total darkness of night being the best times to troll.

On big water, trolling catches more walleyes per hour than any other fishing technique. These anglers are using a mast system to spread their lures behind and to the sides of their boat.

lakes and rivers, and is typically found over rocky reefs and shoals of gravel, bedrock, and other firm bottoms.

But in the Great Lakes and large, northern lakes and western reservoirs, walleyes can also be found miles from any significant bottom structure, roaming wide-open expanses of water in search of prey fish. These nomadic schools, sometimes miles long and wide, suspend in the water column below baitfish. As a result, this behavior of roaming open water makes walleyes particularly vulnerable to trolling.

Spring Spawning

A walleye's year begins in the early spring. At ice-out in northern climates, with water temperatures edging near the 40-degree mark, male walleyes move to spawning reefs in lakes or ascend rivers in anticipation of the larger females arriving to breed. Walleyes don't build and guard nests as do bass and some other fish species. Instead, the females deposit their thousands of eggs across the bottom near suitable substrate such as rocks, gravel, and cobble. As they do, males immediately swim alongside the females and eject their white sperm to

Why Troll for Walleyes? These Two Charts Tell the Story on Lake Erie

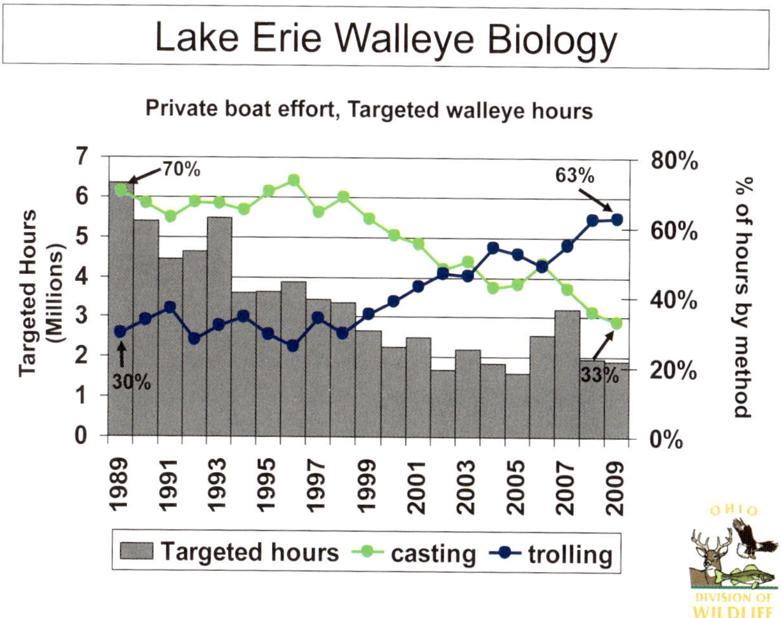

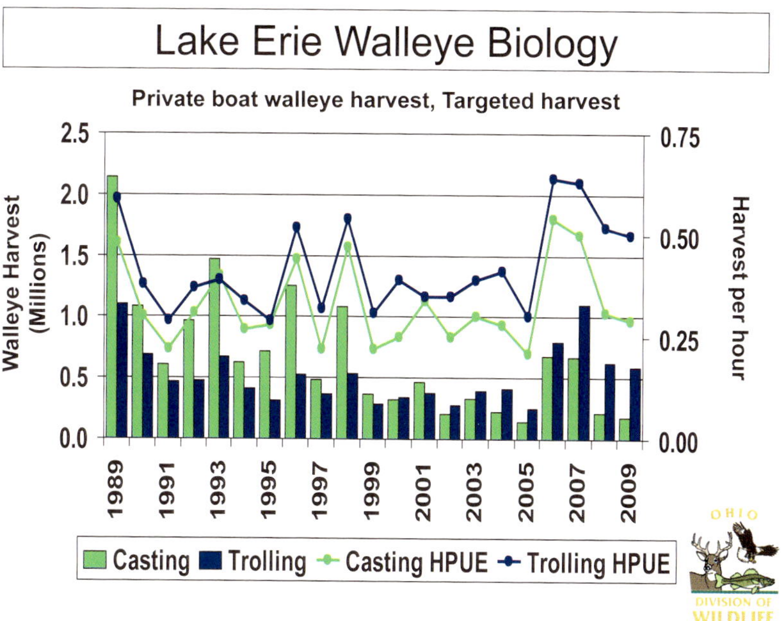

HPUE=Harvest Per Unit of Effort. Charts Courtesy of the Ohio Department of Natural Resources, Division of Wildlife.

fertilize the eggs. No parental care is given the eggs nor the fry once the eggs hatch. The young walleye are simply on their own in a very hostile underwater world where few young fish survive to adulthood, possibly only one in a thousand.

This type of spawning behavior—known as broadcast spawning—may seem like a wasteful process, but many other fish and aquatic animals benefit from eating walleye eggs. There is no waste in nature. Walleye spawning may continue for a month or more, until the water temperature reaches about 55 degrees. As a result, not all the walleyes in a particular body of water spawn at the same time, helping ensure survival of the species. For instance, if eggs deposited early in the spring are blown off a spawning reef by a storm and destroyed, eggs deposited later may survive and hatch.

After the spawn, adult walleyes need time to recover, particularly the large females. They leave their spawning reefs or river shallows and lie on the bottom in deep water, inactive, possibly for days. During that time, fishing for walleyes can be tough, but once they have rested, walleyes become ravenous, and anglers can experience some of the best fishing of the year.

In the Great Lakes and most large lakes and rivers, walleyes are migratory, not only following schools of baitfish as they move but also seeking comfortable water temperatures. As waters warm in late spring and early summer, large walleyes, in particular, seek cooler conditions. This explains, for example, why it's difficult to catch a trophy walleye in Lake Erie's Western Basin during the heat of late summer, but is comparatively easy during the cooler waters of early spring. Leaving the relatively shallow Western Basin, the fish move north and east, seeking the cooler, deeper waters on the Canadian side of the lake, or they swim as far as 100 miles or more east to the deeper and cooler conditions in Lake Erie's Central Basin.

Summertime, and the Living Is Easy

No matter where walleyes swim in North America, they spend the summer gorging themselves on baitfish. As water temperatures continue to rise, their body metabolism ramps up and they literally become eating machines, feeding nearly 24 hours per day. That's what makes summer walleye fishing so productive. The fish are hungry, so no matter when you go fishing, night or day, the catching is usually good. The only exception to that rule would be fishing during a severe cold front or immediately following a wind storm that has churned the water, making it turbid. But even then the poor fishing is usually short-lived, as a walleye's body demands food during summer and lots of it.

By late summer and early fall, a walleye fisherman has added competition to deal with, and I'm not talking about other anglers. Millions upon millions of small fish of many species have hatched by that time of year, and walleyes have a veritable choice of foods, a literal smorgasbord, and they don't have to make much of an effort to get it. As a result, fishing can lull for a month or two. There is simply too much other food in the lake for a walleye to swim out of its way to take your bait.

Fall Fishing

By fall, walleyes are already beginning to feel the instinctual urges forcing them back toward their spring spawning grounds. Catch and filet an adult female walleye late in the fall, and you will see her

A Great Lakes charter boat heads out for a day of walleye fishing. Successful trolling is a combination of thorough equipment preparation and precise trolling technique. Remember, details matter.

egg sac already beginning to develop. Dropping water temperatures trigger the start of this fall migration toward the spawning area. The journey is a leisurely one, however, with the fish being in no hurry to get there. This is what can make fall walleye fishing so unbelievably productive. Find a large, staging school of walleyes and that school may stay in the same area for weeks. Lake Erie has such a place—as do most large lakes—a 15-mile stretch of water near the south shore from Huron to Vermilion, Ohio. Large fish cruise this area, known as "The Bowl" because of its rounded, bowl-like shape, in autumn by the thousands, and the fishing can be fantastic for trophy walleyes.

The Late Fall to Winter Transition

Open-water walleye fishing can be very productive right up until ice formation no longer allows trolling. But fishermen need to judge weather conditions carefully during this time of year, as more and more storms arrive in advance of winter. As a result, the water cools rapidly and high winds can make for treacherous boating conditions on big water. No walleye, not even a trophy fish, is worth endangering your life or the lives of your fishing buddies, so beware the weather in fall. But if conditions are relatively calm, and you are properly dressed for the cold, by all means go fishing. Some of the largest walleyes of the year are caught trolling just before ice covers the lakes.

When ice and snow finally seal the surface of North America's northern lakes and rivers, a walleye's year quietly comes to an end. The fish can still be caught by ice fishing, but because of the colder water temperatures a walleye's metabolism is the slowest it will be for the entire year. Consequently, walleyes eat relatively little while under the ice compared to other times of the year, and as a result are more difficult to catch.

How Long Do Walleyes Live?

Walleyes repeat the annual cycle just described every year of their lives. How long do they live? Fishery biologists used to believe that walleyes were relatively short-lived fish, growing rapidly but living at the most about 10 to 12 years. This thinking was based on aging walleyes by using scale samples; the microscopic rings on a fish scale were counted under a microscope, much like growth rings on a tree stump.

State Record Walleyes

Walleye Central

More Walleye Information Than You Can Handle

Courtesy of Walleye Central (www.walleyecentral.com)

Alabama	10 lbs, 14 oz	1980	Weiss Lake
Arizona	16 lbs, 1.76 oz	2002	Show Low Lake
Arkansas	22 lbs, 11 oz ***	1982	Greers Ferry Lake
Colorado	18 lbs, 13 oz	1997	Standley Lake
Connecticut	14 lbs, 8 oz	1941	Candlewood Lake
Georgia	11 lbs, 6 oz	1995	Richard B. Russell Lake
Idaho	17 lbs, 9.6 oz	2006	Salmon Falls Creek Reservoir
Illinois	14 lbs	1961	Kankakee River
Indiana	14 lbs, 4 oz *	1977	Tippecanoe River
Iowa	14 lbs, 7.75 oz	1986	Des Moines River
Kansas	13 lbs, 10.56 oz	1996	Wilson Reservoir
Kentucky	21 lbs, 8 oz	1958	Lake Cumberland
Maine	5 lbs, 12.8 oz	2010	Messalonskee Lake
Maryland	14 lbs, 4 oz	1998	Jennings Randolph Reservoir
Massachusetts	11 lbs	1975	Quabbin Reservoir
Michigan	17 lbs, 3.04 oz	1951	Pine River
Minnesota	17 lbs, 8 oz	1979	Seagull River
Mississippi	9 lbs, 10 oz	1985	Tennessee River
Montana	17 lbs, 12 oz	2007	Lake Elwell
Nebraska	16 lbs, 2 oz	1971	Lake McConaughy
Nevada	14 lbs, 14 oz	1992	Rye Patch Reservoir
New Hampshire	12 lbs, 8.8 oz	1992	Connecticut River
New Jersey	13 lbs, 9 oz	1993	Delaware River
New Mexico	16 lbs, 9 oz	1989	Clayton Lake
New York	16 lbs, 9 oz	2009	Mystic Lake
North Carolina	13 lbs, 8 oz	1986	Lake Chatuge
North Dakota	15 lbs, 12 oz	1959	Wood Lake
Ohio	16 lbs, 3 oz	1999	Lake Erie
Oklahoma	12 lbs, 10 oz	1995	Altus-Lugert Lake
Oregon	19 lbs, 15.3 oz	1990	Columbia River
Pennsylvania	17 lbs, 9 oz	1980	Allegheny Reservoir
South Carolina	10 lbs	1994	Richard B. Russell Lake
South Dakota	16 lbs, 2 oz	2002	Lake Francis Case
Tennessee	25 lbs **	1960	Old Hickory Reservoir
Texas	11 lbs, 14.08 oz	1990	Lake Meredith
Utah	15 lbs, 9 oz	1991	Provo River
Vermont	13 lbs, 4 oz	1993	Lower Clyde River
Virginia	17 lbs, 13.12 oz	2003	Kanawha Falls
Washington	19 lbs, 4.8 oz	2007	Columbia River
West Virginia	18 lbs, 15.52 oz	2004	Elk River
Wisconsin	18 lbs	1933	High Lake
Wyoming	17 lbs, 6.72 oz	1991	Boysen Reservoir

**Tied a previous record*

***Disallowed as the world record by the National Fresh Water Fishing Hall of Fame*

****Current world record*

In recent years, however, biologists have developed a much more accurate way of aging various species of fish, walleyes included. By counting the growth rings on a fish's otolith—a dish-shaped, inner-ear bone—walleyes have been determined to live as much as twice as long as previously thought. This revelation has been invaluable information for fishery managers and biologists, in some cases changing the thinking about long-held fish management practices and altering the decisions made by state and federal fishery agencies.

In short, what this new information means for fishermen is that walleyes should be treated and respected as the prized natural resource they are. This is especially true of trophy walleyes, fish that may have lived 20 years or longer. Walleye fishing regulations are enacted first, to protect the fishery resource, and second, to spread the harvest of that walleye resource among as many fishermen as possible. Being an ethical angler—obeying the fishing regulations—ensures the future of walleye fishing. I have kids and grandkids that I'd like to have the same opportunities I've had to go walleye fishing. How about you. . . . ?

Chapter 2

What You'll Need

Basic Walleye Trolling Equipment

Several years ago, a close friend of mine bought a new boat and asked me to teach him how to troll for walleyes on the Great Lakes. I was glad to show him the ropes, as he and I had grown up together, spending many memorable days afield fishing and hunting. But when he started asking specific questions about tackle, techniques, and tactics, I was reminded just how confusing the world of walleye trolling can be for a newcomer. In essence, it was the germ of an idea that led to the writing of this book.

If you're a novice to walleye trolling, the basic information in this chapter will help get you started. Just remember to keep things as simple as possible when beginning. For example, learn to troll with just one rod per side of the boat before adding a second, third, or possibly even more. Learning one piece of gear and one technique at a time, and then adding to that as you become proficient, is preferable to trying to take on too much too fast.

Walleye trolling, if done right, is both art and science—a combination of knowledge and technical skills—and it all takes time to learn. Attempt too much too soon, and you'll not only become frustrated, but will likely make a tangled mess of your tackle, as well. Remember, fishing is supposed to be fun. Don't rush the learning curve.

Rods

Most serious walleye anglers on the Great Lakes use seven- to eight-foot trolling rods with a medium or medium-heavy action. Rods need to have enough backbone not only to control heavy fish, but also to handle diving devices and/or inline planer boards, which we'll discuss in Chapter Three. Graphite is not necessary in trolling rods—or at least not much of it—as the fish hook themselves, so you don't need the "feel" of a sensitive, high-dollar rod.

All walleye trolling rods aboard your boat should be identical, and matched with identical line-counter reels. The rods should be placed in solidly mounted rod holders while trolling.

That said, I recommend either fiberglass trolling rods or rods with only a minimal amount of graphite content. These rods are more forgiving than rods with high-graphite content, meaning they're less brittle and less likely to break under stress or rough use. And make no mistake, trolling is tough on tackle. In addition, fiberglass or low-graphite-content rods help act as a shock absorber to the line when a fish hits, and also during the fight. This is especially important if you're trolling a braided superline, which has virtually no stretch.

An inexpensive trolling rod that does the job very well is a Shakespeare Ugly Stik, model CA 1100 (seven-foot, medium action). I was so impressed with these rods when I first began using them aboard a buddy's boat that I now use them on my own.

When purchasing trolling rods, it's important to have all your rods match, meaning all the rods should be of the same manufacture, length, and action. Matching rods can be quickly interchanged in a trolling spread. Also, if you place rod holders side by side, you can easily tell if one rod has a fish on it—even a small fish—as the rod tip will be bent slightly more than the others. This signals that the bait or lure needs to be checked and the small fish removed. If you don't know that a fish is there, you could drag it behind the boat for a half hour or more, not only killing the fish, but also making that particular bait unavailable for a walleye. In short, trolling with a mishmash of rods and rod actions makes your job more difficult than it need be, and you won't be as successful, as a result. Spend the extra money for matching rods; you'll be glad you did.

Reels

Once you catch a walleye at a certain depth while trolling, being able to place your lure or bait back to that same, exact depth of water is critical. Level-wind, line-counter reels allow you to do just that. These specialized reels have a small readout meter built into them that tells how much line, usually calculated in feet, is being let out.

Russ Clark, a charter captain on Lake Michigan, suggests using line-counter reels with a high gear ratio, at least 4:1: "They help get lines to the boat quicker, as lines can be a long way out at times." And just as with your trolling rods, it's important to have all of your reels match. That way, there is no confusion as to how a reel works when a fish hits and it's time for action.

There are several brands of line-counter reels on the market that will do the job well. Buy any of the top brands—Daiwa, Okuma, Shimano—and you will likely be well satisfied. Just remember to purchase the best-quality reels you can afford. I once had a dairy farmer friend of mine comment, "I can't afford to buy cheap cows." He knew that inexpensive livestock would cost him more money in the long run. The same is true with fishing tackle; buy cheap rods and reels, and you'll likely be replacing that equipment sooner rather than later. And inexpensive tackle will also not work as well as quality-made equipment, costing you fish and frustration.

Personally, I use Daiwa Sealine SG27LCA line-counter reels. These workhorse reels have been on my trolling rods for years, and I've yet to experience a problem with any of them.

Lines

Stroll the aisles of any tackle shop, particularly the big-box stores, and you'll be overwhelmed by the number of fishing line choices available. To help keep your choice simple for walleye trolling, the main line should be either monofilament or braid, also known as superline.

Longtime, professional walleye angler Mark Brumbaugh of Arcanum, Ohio, prefers trolling 10-pound test monofilament in the cold

Fish on! The angler on the right is reeling in a walleye caught on a crankbait trolled behind an inline planer board. The location is Munuscong Lake in Michigan's Upper Peninsula.

water of spring, believing that the extra stretch in the line hooks more fish. "Walleyes are less aggressive in spring, and I've had more hook-ups using mono as opposed to braid," he said. "It's not that the fish are seeing the braid and being spooked. I believe it has more to do with the elasticity of the mono itself."

Personally, I prefer to troll year-round with braid (Berkley FireLine, 20-pound test), but I also fish for fun, not for dollars as does Brumbaugh. Because braid does not stretch, it transfers more of what's happening at the end of the line to the rod. Braid also works better than mono when using diving devices, such as Luhr Jensen Dipsy Divers, making for a crisper release of the diving device when a fish hits or when you have to trip a diver's release manually. But more about that in the next chapter.

Leaders

Most walleye fishermen attach a leader to the end of their main trolling line, whether that main line is monofilament or braid. I use 20-pound test Seaguar fluorocarbon leader material, cut into six-foot lengths. By the time I tie either a swivel or snap-swivel to each end of the leader, it's down to about five and a half feet in length. Tying a knot in each end of the leader—which is unavoidable—weakens the leader slightly, so I'm really fishing with about a 17- to 18-pound test leader, which is why I chose 20-pound test to begin with. And I like fluorocarbon as opposed to monofilament leaders because fluorocarbon is virtually invisible underwater.

As to leader length, the thing to remember is not to make your leaders any longer than your trolling rods. If you do, you won't be able to reel them up far enough to land a fish, because the snap-swivel on the leader will not pass through the tip-top line guide of the rod. When walleyes are really finicky, some tournament pros do make their leaders longer than their rods, possibly as long as 10 feet or more. Just keep in mind that if you ever try this stealth technique, you'll have to walk toward the bow of your boat to land a fish while your fishing buddy nets the walleye from the transom.

It's also important to check leaders regularly for nicks and cuts. This should be done between fishing trips at least, and more often if you are fishing around rocks or other places where sharp-edged objects could cut leaders. The small zebra and Quagga mussels that have invaded the Great Lakes in recent years have extremely sharp shell edges, so beware. An easy way to check a leader for minute nicks is to run the leader between your thumb and index finger. If you feel even the slightest irregularity, replace the leader.

Lures

When selecting lures for big-water walleye trolling, crankbaits and nightcrawler-harness spinner rigs can be used all through the open-water period of the year, spring through fall. Spoons are most productive during the warm-water summer months. During cold-water periods (spring and fall), walleyes want a more subtle-action bait, which is what most large, medium-action crankbaits and spinner rigs provide. In warmer water, high-action lures attract walleyes better, which is why spoons and high-action crankbaits work well in summer.

Spoons are my favorite summertime trolling lure, with high-action crankbaits such as Reef Runners or Rapala Deep Tail Dancers being my second choice. For colors of spoons—at least for Lake Erie—it's hard to beat hammered gold, with hammered copper a close second. But don't be afraid to try spoons of other colors, especially spoons with a touch of pink or purple. Spoons with copper-colored backs are usually more productive for walleyes than spoons with silver backs.

Crankbaits can be trolled productively all season, from early spring through late fall. Just remember to slow them down during the cool-water periods of the year and speed them up in summer.

Walleyes chase spoons because the twisting and fluttering of these lures imitate an injured baitfish. Just make sure you are trolling thin, flutter-type spoons. Spoons made for casting or jigging are heavier, and don't provide as much action to the lure when trolled.

My favorite trolling spoons are Michigan Stingers: Light Scorpion size (2.25 inches) for smaller fish, and Stinger size (3.75 inches) for larger walleyes. Stinger also makes a Stingray size (4.25 inches) and Magnum Stinger (4.75 inches), which are mainly salmon-sized

Chip's Walleye Trolling Tackle

The following is a list of the brand-name walleye trolling tackle I personally use, from boat to baits. Other quality equipment will work well, too. This is simply reliable, time-tested gear that has consistently put walleyes in the boat for me, year after year.

Boat and motor: Yar-Craft (1785 Cobra DC) with a Yamaha 115 hp four-stroke outboard

Electronics: Lowrance

Rod holders: Bert's Custom Tackle

Rods: Shakespeare Ugly Stik, model CA 1100

Reels: Daiwa Sealine SG27LCA (line-counter)

Line: Berkley FireLine (20-pound test, 8-pound diameter, smoke color)

Leader material: Seaguar fluorocarbon (20-pound test)

Inline planer boards: Off Shore Tackle, OR12L (left) and OR12R (right) with OR18 Snapper Clips

Diving Devices: Luhr Jensen Dipsy Divers and Jet Divers, Big Jon Mini-Disks

Favorite Crankbaits: Reef Runner (Deep Diver and Ripstick), Rapala Husky Jerk, Smithwick Rattlin' Rogue, Rapala Tail Dancer

Spoons: Michigan Stinger, Scorpion (2.25 inches), and Stinger (3.75 inches)

Nightcrawler-Harness Spinner Rigs: Homemade with 30-pound test monofilament line tied to three #2 bait-holder Eagle Claw hooks, and a single, holographic gold blade (size 5 or 6)

Landing net: StowMaster, model TS108S (handle extends to nine feet)

spoons, but can also be used for targeting large walleyes. Trolling these larger spoons can also help keep small, non-target fish from hitting your lures.

Speed

How fast should you troll for walleyes? In general, think cold water versus warm water, with somewhere around 55 to 60 degrees usually being the change-over point. Ice-out, early-spring crankbait trolling,

Night crawler harnesses can be as simple as two or three hooks and a single spinner blade. They should be trolled slowly, no more than 0.5 to about 1.5 miles per hour.

with water temperature in the 30s, should begin at about 1 mile per hour or even less. At times, 0.5 to 0.8 mph is not too slow in very cold water. On some days you may even have to take your boat out of gear and stop crankbaits dead in the water for a few seconds to coax a bite. As the water warms in spring, gradually increase your speed to 1.5 to possibly 2 miles per hour. This added speed will give your lures more action.

Once the water warms to about 60 degrees and above, spoons come into their own. These high-action lures should be pulled at 2 to 2.5 miles per hour to take full advantage of their capabilities. In late summer, when water temperature is at its peak for the year, spoons can even be "burned" up to 3 miles per hour. An advantage of pulling them that fast is that it can sometimes help keep undesirable, non-target fish from hitting them.

Nightcrawler-harness spinner rigs can be trolled fast, too—2 miles per hour or even faster—and still catch fish, but mainly they're considered a slower, stealthier bait presentation and are usually pulled at an average 1.5 miles per hour. Nightcrawler harnesses are good baits to troll during a cold front when fish are less aggressive, as the scent of the worm helps entice walleyes to bite.

A single, Colorado blade is used on most nightcrawler-harness spinner rigs, and a size five is an average-sized blade for fishing big water. Willow leaf blades, being slimmer, can be trolled a bit faster than Colorado blades, say two miles per hour, and are a good choice when covering large areas of water searching for fish.

Choosing colors of spinner blades for walleyes is similar to choosing colors of spoons: you can't go wrong with gold, at least to start. And spinner rigs with quick-change clevises allow you to change blade size and color easily. Every day on the water is different, so don't be afraid to experiment with color and speed no matter what lure or bait you pull behind the boat.

Trolling Bags

Since walleye trolling is a relatively slow-motion affair—three miles per hour tops, and usually much slower—what do you do if you don't have a boat motor that can troll that slowly? Trolling bags, also known as sea anchors or trolling socks, are the answer. These devices are funnel-shaped bags, open at both ends, and usually made of nylon or canvas. They attach to opposite sides of a boat from the front gunnel

Trolling bags, also known as drift socks or sea anchors, help slow a boat to trolling speed. Usually made of nylon or canvas, they are tied to a gunnel cleat on each side of the boat.

cleats and slow a boat's forward progress by forcing water through the bag. Electric trolling motors and small, gas-powered outboard "kicker" motors are an alternative for slowing your boat's speed, but trolling bags are much more inexpensive than purchasing a second motor, and there's little to no maintenance. However, having a second motor on your boat is insurance that, should your main motor not start or fail to work properly for any reason, you'll still get back to the dock.

We'll get into more advanced walleye trolling tackle and equipment in the next chapter, but the main thing to remember when first assembling your basic rods, reels, lines, leaders, and lures is to buy quality equipment. Do so, and you'll have tackle that will not only last for years, but will put many more walleyes in the boat for you in the meantime.

Chapter 3

Down and Out

Advanced Walleye Trolling Equipment

Walleyes are usually easier to catch when they're in shallow water, for two reasons. First, they're more easily located, and second, they're more likely to be actively feeding. But except during spring spawning season, walleyes are seldom in shallow water. Rather, they instinctively prefer the mid to bottom depths of a body of water. It's just the nature of the critter. The question for the walleye angler then becomes how to get lures and baits to those lower levels of the water column, and what lures and baits work best most often?

As I discussed in the previous chapter, summer walleyes love spoons, and a basic question from new walleye trollers is how to get those thin, lightweight spoons down to depth, where the fish are. The answer is a diving device. Many are on the market, but one of the most popular, which has been catching walleyes for decades, is the Luhr Jensen Dipsy Diver.

Dipsy Divers

A Dipsy Diver not only takes a spoon or other lure—such as a nightcrawler harness or shallow-lipped crankbait—down in the water column, but it can also make the lure run out to the side of the boat. And there is a definite advantage to a lure tracking to the side of your boat as opposed to directly behind it. Walleyes are timid fish and easily spooked by the presence of a boat and motor, especially in shallow water. By running baits to the side, any walleyes spooked by the boat and swimming laterally away from it will encounter your lures.

Dipsy Divers and other similar diving devices accomplish this "sideshow" by offsetting a built-in lead weight on the base plate of the diver. There are four settings on a Dipsy Diver base plate (0, 1, 2, 3), and by adjusting the weight to different settings you can choose to troll directly behind the boat (0 setting) or as much as at a 45-degree angle to the side of the boat (3 setting).

An assortment of Luhr Jensen Dipsy Divers attached to identical trolling rods. Notice the colored rubber "snubbers," tied between the divers and the leaders, to help lessen the shock when a fish hits. Snubbers are primarily used for salmon and steelhead fishing, but can also be used for walleye trolling.

A series of Dipsy Divers can even be trolled at different depths (vertically) and at different distances and angles from the boat (horizontally) by adjusting the individual divers to different settings. Using this technique, you can literally comb the water column from top to bottom for walleyes. And when the fish begin to hit some of your lures but not others, the unproductive lures can then be adjusted to the more productive depth. In other words, by spreading lures both horizontally and vertically behind your boat, you let the walleyes tell you at what depth they are holding and what lure(s) they like on a particular day. We'll talk more about the details of creating effective trolling spreads in the next chapter.

To attach Dipsy Divers or other trolling devices to your main trolling line use a sturdy, large snap-swivel. Don't scrimp on quality here. Because of their relatively large surface area, Dipsy Divers pull through the water heavily, and you don't want one breaking off because you used a poorly made (as in cheap) snap-swivel that couldn't take the stress. Most diving devices cost around $10 each, so you don't want to lose one inadvertently. And between fishing trips, remember to retie the knot on your main line that holds the snap-swivel that holds the diving device, as knots weaken over time.

Dipsy Divers come in four sizes and achieve dive depths from 20 to 100 feet. Most walleye anglers use size 0 or size 1 Dipsy Divers. I use a combination of size 0 (for running lures shallower) and size 1 (for running lures deeper). Both sizes come equipped with a removable, plastic outer ring that increases the surface area of the diving device. By leaving the ring in place, the device dives deeper with less line out. Remove the ring, and it takes more line out to achieve the same depth. This can be an advantage if you want to run your divers farther from the boat to avoid spooking fish. The devices come with a handy depth chart that tells you how much line to let out to achieve certain trolling depths, both with or without a ring attached.

Dipsy Divers also have a moveable arm that must be snapped into place before lowering the device into the water. An adjustable set screw controls the tension that holds the arm, and should be set to release at about two to three pounds of pressure. The arm needs to release easily when a fish hits, but not be set so lightly that it releases prematurely when the boat surges forward under normal wave action while trolling. The more you work with this type of diving device, the more you'll get the feel of the proper pressure needed.

As you let the Dipsy Diver down into the water column, apply tension to the trolling line. This can be accomplished by either applying

A Luhr Jensen Dipsy Diver arm should be set to release at about two to three pounds of pressure. Tightening or loosening the set screw with a screwdriver easily accomplishes this task.

thumb pressure to the reel spool or setting your line-counter reel's alarm clicker to the "on" position. If a Dipsy Diver is not under tension during its descent, it may spin and tangle around the main line or leader and not work properly once it's in fishing position.

Dipsy Divers come in various colors, and two schools of thought prevail as to which colors to choose for walleye fishing: subtle or bold. When fishing with spoons, which are high-action lures, I prefer either solid gold or solid silver colored Dipsies. My thinking is that I want the diver to reflect as much light as possible as it moves through the water, hoping that walleyes will think it's a school of baitfish and be attracted to the flash from long distances. Once the fish move in for a closer look, they then see a single, struggling minnow (the spoon) trailing behind the Dipsy and hopefully strike it.

On the other hand, walleye anglers who fish night crawler–harness spinner rigs behind Dipsy Divers want just the opposite effect. Since spinner rigs are considered a more stealthy presentation and usually are fished more slowly than spoons (on average about 1.5 miles per hour for night crawler–harness spinner rigs as opposed to about 2.0 to 2.5 miles per hour for spoons), these anglers want their Dipsies to be as unobtrusive as possible. Consequently, their choice of Dipsy Diver colors is usually either clear or flat black.

But no matter what color Dipsy Diver you choose, they all work the same when a fish hits. The arm that holds the planer at an angle in the water releases, allowing you to fight the fish without the encumbrance of the diving device pulling it downward.

I attach a five- to six-foot fluorocarbon leader to my Dipsy Divers, again using a quality snap-swivel. The lure is then attached to the end of the leader by another snap-swivel or possibly just a snap. A snap is lighter than a snap-swivel and will not deaden the action of a lure quite as much. I use a snap when attaching crankbaits to the end of a leader, but a snap-swivel when attaching spoons, as a snap-swivel helps prevent line twist with the high-action spoons.

Jet Divers

Another diving device, especially popular on Lake Erie because of the lake's relatively shallow depths, is the rocket-shaped Luhr Jensen Jet Diver. Unlike Dipsy Divers, Jet Divers are not directional, so must be trolled behind inline planer boards or mast systems to make them run to the side of your boat.

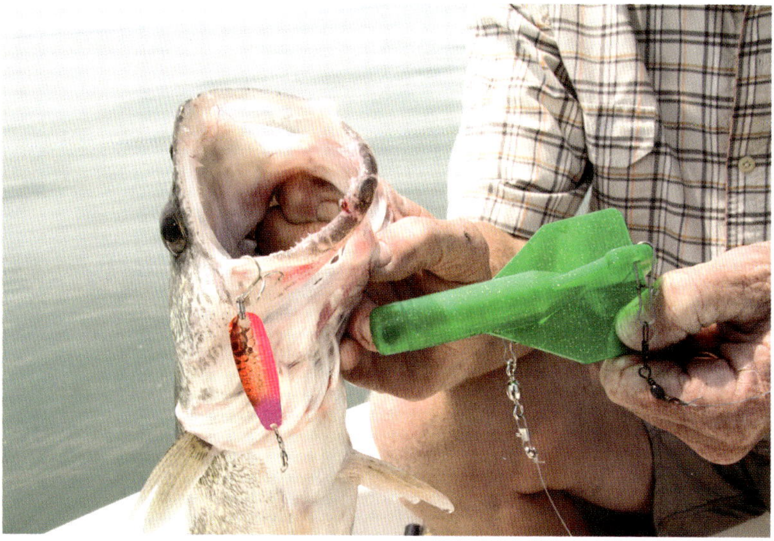

The combination of a Luhr Jensen Jet Diver and a small, colored spoon enticed this Lake Erie walleye. Spoons are high-action lures that should be trolled between two and three miles per hour during the time of year when water is warmest.

There are five sizes of Jet Divers (10, 20, 30, 40, and 50), the number indicating approximately how deep the device will dive with an adequate amount of line out. When purchasing Jet Divers, keep in mind that larger sizes can be fished shallower by letting out less line, and smaller sizes can be fished deeper by letting out more line. A good compromise is size 20, 30, or 40.

Attach a Jet Diver to your main line the same as you would a Dipsy Diver, with a quality snap-swivel. A fluorocarbon leader then attaches to the rear of the Jet, and a lure attaches to the end of the leader. Jet Divers take a lure down in the water column when trolled, due to the planing angle built into the diving device. When a fish hits, the weight and pull of the fish cause the Jet Diver to roll over, so the device no longer planes downward. The fish can then be fought to the boat without the encumbrance of the diver.

Keep in mind that Jet Divers are buoyant and float when not being trolled. Dipsy Divers, on the other hand, sink when not being trolled. This is good information to know should you ever have to take your boat motor out of gear for some reason and shift into neutral. Since Dipsy Divers sink, you may want to reel them in before stopping the boat. If you don't, and you're trolling over a rocky bottom, you could get snagged and lose a diver.

Den Braun

Den Braun of Vermilion, Ohio, is an expert on Lake Erie Central Basin walleye trolling. An ex-charter captain, he also once owned a bait and tackle shop, so he knows diving devices. "Jet Divers used to be mainly a summer and early-fall technique, when the lake water was warmest," said Braun. "But now, like a lot of presentations, guys are starting to use Jets all the time when they find walleyes suspended in the water column."

Braun continued, "Sizes 20, 30, and 40 are the most popular on Erie, but one of the most common misconceptions about Jet Divers is that anglers think the size corresponds to the deepest depth the diver will go. The trolling manual *Precision Trolling (Big Water Edition)* by Michigan outdoor writer Mark Romanack blew that belief out of the water. For instance, you can get a size 10 Jet Diver down to as much as 25 or 30 feet, depending upon the diameter of line you're trolling and how much line you let out. Jets are a lot more versatile than most guys think."

Braun went on to say that most Erie trollers use four- to six-foot leaders behind their Jets. Twenty-pound test leader material should be adequate for about any walleye, and at the same time be able to

Diving devices need not be large to get the job done, especially when walleyes are relatively shallow. This Big Jon mini-disk, about the size of a 50-cent piece, took a colored spoon down far enough in the water column to help catch this limit of walleyes.

handle a stray steelhead or other powerful game fish that just might hit your lure. But don't be afraid to go to a lighter leader if fish become finicky, especially in clear water.

Another concern in clear water is the color of the Jet Diver itself. Braun believes that too bright a color may actually spook walleyes. His opinion is that a clear or black-colored Jet, or at least a flat finish, usually produces more fish.

On Erie, most walleye anglers run small spoons behind their Jet Divers, such as Michigan Stinger Scorpions (2.25 inches) or regular Stingers (3.75 inches). Other productive spoon brands include Pa's Fintail, Silver Leaf, and Silver Streak. Lipless crankbaits or spinner-crawler combinations are also used occasionally. When running multiple rods, Jet Divers are usually spread behind the boat with the help of inline planer boards.

Mark Courts

Mark Courts of Harris, Minnesota, is a walleye pro who trolled Jet Divers successfully in Lake Erie's Central Basin during a tournament out of Cleveland several years ago. "I run 6/14 Berkley FireLine on my reels, which is so thin in diameter that with 100 feet of line out size 20 Jets will dive to 30 feet and 30 Jets will go as deep as 40 feet," he said. "During the Cleveland tournament, I ran two Jet Divers on my outside lines on inline planer boards and two lead-core lines on the inside. I either buy black Jet Divers or spray paint them black, so as not to spook fish. But there are some days when I believe colored divers actually attract walleyes."

Courts likes to run double willow-leaf night crawler harnesses off his Jets, and he prefers tipping them with a Berkley Gulp! or Berkley PowerBait artificial night crawler as opposed to a real worm. "During the Cleveland tournament, I was catching 40 to 50 walleyes a day, and a single artificial crawler could catch up to half a dozen fish before I had to replace it," Courts said. "That made me more efficient. By not having to put on a live night crawler after every fish, I increased my fishing time."

Ernie Olson

Another Minnesota pro who fishes a lot with lead-core line is Ernie Olson. If you're unfamiliar with lead-core trolling line, it's exactly what

Lead-core line is marked every 30 feet (10 yards) with a different color. Heavier than other trolling lines, lead-core allows anglers to get baits and lures deeper in the water column quicker and with less line out.

it sounds like, a line that contains a lead center, covered by an outer sheathing. As a result, lead-core line is heavy, taking lures and baits to depth quicker than other lines. The advantage of using lead-core for walleye trolling is that you don't have to let out as much line to achieve the desired depth.

"I segment my lead-core, using 20-pound test monofilament above the lead and 20 feet of 14- to 17-pound test monofilament below the lead," said Olson. "I usually have half a dozen rods aboard my boat holding anywhere from six to 10 colors of lead-core."

To explain, one "color" of lead-core line measures 10 yards or 30 feet. The line is marked with a different color every 10 yards so that anglers know precisely how much line they are letting out for any particular trolling situation.

One of Olson's favorite lures to troll with lead-core line is a Renosky stickbait. Of the two sizes available, he prefers the larger Renosky. He modifies the lure by removing all three of the original treble hooks and replacing the back two with extra large, #2 red Mustad hooks. But he does not replace the front hook, believing that leaving it off gives the bait a harder wobble. His favorite colors on sunny days are clown and chartreuse, and on cloudy days purple and dark blue. His Renosky baits must also have an orange belly.

“If they don’t already have an orange belly, I’ll take a permanent marker and put one on,” Olson said. “I also always add half a night crawler to the back hook. Always. And I look to see where my fish are hooked when I land them. If they are consistently hooked only by the back hook—in other words, if they’re not T-boning my bait and getting both hooks in their mouth—I’ll move the crawler to the front hook and also shorten the length of the crawler.”

Planer Boards

One way of spreading a series of lines and lures horizontally behind a boat is to use planer boards. On larger boats, mast systems with “skis” are usually used, but most anglers with smaller boats use inline planer boards. Inlines are less expensive than a mast system and easier to use. You can also relocate to another fishing spot quicker with inline boards than with the larger mast systems. Here’s how inline planer boards work.

Attach a lure to the end of your line and let it out behind the boat a set distance, say 50 feet according to the readout on your line-counter reel. Next, snap an inline planer board onto the line. Most inline boards have two snap attachments, one at the front of the board and a second at the rear. Run the line through both. Now, place the planer

If you own a larger boat, a mast system can pull “skis” rather than inline planer boards.

Getting Down with Three-Ways

Another technique used for getting walleye baits down in the water column is to employ a three-way swivel rig. In essence, a large-billed crankbait—such as a Reef Runner Deep Diver or Rapala Deep Tail Dancer—becomes a diving planer by being tied from a six-foot leader to the bottom loop of a three-way swivel. Above that, a four-foot leader is tied to the middle loop of the three-way. A second bait is then attached to the shorter leader, usually a spoon or spinner-crawler harness. Where legal, this rig doubles your chances of getting a bite, because you have twice as many lures in the water.

board in the water, and as you let line out the board will begin to track to the side of the boat—the distance determined by how much line you give it. The lure is then pulled along behind the planer board. *This is important:* when buying inline planer boards, be aware there are port side (left) and starboard side (right) boards. Buy the same number of boards for each side of the boat. If you're just beginning to learn walleye trolling, a total of four to six inline planer boards should be about right, two or three per side.

Once the planer board is as far out as you want it, place the rod in a rod holder, set the reel clicker alarm button to "on," and you're fishing. When a walleye hits, you'll either hear the reel clicker sound, see the planer board begin to wobble side to side in the water, or both. When you do, simply remove the rod from the holder, reel in the line to the planer board, remove the planer board from the line by opening the two snap clips, and fight the fish the remainder of the way to the net.

This procedure may sound complicated, but once you see it done it really isn't. And two anglers working together can accomplish this maneuver faster and easier than one working alone. It's a kind of "dance" you and your fishing partner learn over time until it becomes second nature. Just remember to keep the line taught while removing a planer board or the fish could get off the hook.

And speaking of fish coming unhooked, here's a tip that will get you an extra walleye every once in a while. If you ever see a hit and a miss—meaning you see an inline planer board wobble in the water or pulled back a few feet but then the fish comes off the hook—immediately take that particular rod from its rod holder and walk toward the back of the boat. This maneuver will cause the lure on that line to slow or possibly even completely stop for a few seconds, which is often just enough time for the walleye to hit it again.

Chairman of the Boards

When anglers unfamiliar with walleye trolling go fishing with me for the first time, they often ask how I know a fish is on the line before they do. The secret is to watch the inline planer boards as they track through the water, as well as the tips of your trolling rods. While fishing, I usually have someone else drive my boat so that I can concentrate on watching the lines for a hit. My eyes are constantly scanning back and forth from one side of the boat to the other.

When a fish strikes, the inline planer board attached to that particular line will begin to wobble from side to side on the water's surface, and then the weight of the fish will cause the board to start to drop back behind the boat. Simultaneously, the rod with the fish on it will bend its tip more than the other rods on that side of the boat. If it's a bigger walleye, the rod tip may even begin to pulse back and forth. Remember that I strongly suggested in the previous chapter having all of your trolling rods match one another? This is the reason, to better help detect bites.

Inline planer boards large enough for walleye fishing usually have two attachment points, one on the front of the board and a second at the rear. Run the main line through both.

Inline Weights and Snap Weights

Other ways to get lures down in the water column while trolling include using inline weights or snap weights (sometimes also called drop weights). Inline weights attach to the end of the main trolling line by a snap-swivel. A leader and lure then attach to the rear of the inline weight. Snap weights, on the other hand, snap or clip onto the main line anywhere from a few feet in front of a lure to possibly 50 feet or more ahead of it. The distance depends upon how spooky walleyes are on any particular day.

Inline weights and snap weights are more of a stealth presentation than using Dipsy Divers or Jet Divers to take a lure to depth. A selection of weight sizes in one-ounce increments, from one ounce through three ounces, will allow you to adapt to most walleye fishing situations on big water.

Chapter 4

A Season on the Water

Basic Walleye Trolling Techniques and Lure Spreads Throughout the Year

Once you've gathered all your tackle and other gear, it's finally time to hit the water for that first walleye trolling trip. And as I've cautioned in previous chapters, start simple and slow, building your trolling techniques and confidence as you go. For a novice, trying to handle too much trolling gear at once can quickly become overwhelming and discouraging, to say nothing of the tangled mess of rods, reels, and lines you'll have piled on the floor of your boat. Been there, done that.

This chapter will take you through the basics of a typical year of walleye trolling as I do it, from ice-out to ice-up, early spring through late fall. Other anglers may approach their trolling year slightly differently, varying the details somewhat, but in general this is how walleye trolling is done on the Great Lakes and other large bodies of water by most anglers from season to season.

Early Spring: Trolling Large Stickbaits

My heaviest catches of walleyes—pounds per fish—have come in early spring just after ice-out, before walleyes have spawned. In fact, my heaviest walleye ever, 11.7 pounds and pictured on the cover of this book, was caught during a day when my fishing buddy and I were literally dodging ice floes with our boat and trolling lines. On that day, we caught our Ohio limit of March walleyes (four fish each), those eight fish weighing a few ounces shy of a whopping 50 pounds!

How did we do it? In very early spring, trolling large stickbaits—such as Rapala Husky Jerks, Reef Runner Ripsticks, and Smithwick Rattlin' Rogues—is undoubtedly the best way to go. And you want the lures moving through the water painfully slowly, only one mile per hour or even less. In fact, taking your boat completely out of gear

Early spring is the best time of year to catch trophy walleyes. Slowly trolling large stickbaits will do the trick.

and letting the lures come to a complete stop, at times, is what will trigger a strike. Here's how it's done.

First of all, and this goes for all the trolling techniques described in this book, you should troll downwind. It's rare on the Great Lakes that you have a day without any wind to contend with, but it does happen. On those days when the lake is flat, trolling in most any direction is possible, but on windy days, moving directly downwind makes trolling much simpler. By doing so, it's easier to "read" the inline planer boards and rod tips for a bite, and it's also easier to control the boat.

By Ohio law, anglers are allowed to fish with two rods each, so if I'm fishing on Lake Erie in Ohio waters with a partner, that means we can run a total of four lines. I begin the day by selecting four different-colored lures from four different lure manufacturers. Those four different lure brands will each produce a slightly different action and vibration. For instance, I might run a Reef Runner Ripstick (color Bare Naked) on one line, a Smithwick Rattlin' Rogue (color blue and silver) on a second line, a Rapala Husky Jerk (color Firetiger) on a third line, and a Bomber Long A (color gold and silver), on the fourth line. The idea is to have a variety of lure colors and actions in the water, letting the walleyes tell you what they like on a particular day. If one brand or color of lure starts to get hit consistently, I eventually change most or all of my lures over to that brand and color.

In early spring, feeding walleyes will likely be found in the top half of the water column, because that is where the warmest water in a lake will be at that time of year. As a result, I set my lures back behind inline planer boards to cover the depths from a few feet below the surface to about halfway to the bottom. Knowing how deep certain lures dive is critical to placing them precisely in the water column. You can get an accurate idea of a lure's dive curve by referring to the manual *Precision Trolling Pro,* produced by Michigan outdoors writer Mark Romanack. See the sidebar on page 47 for more details about ordering this invaluable trolling tool.

Once I've selected my lures, I let them out behind the boat a specific distance. For instance, if I'm fishing in 20 feet of water, I might put my first lure back 25 feet, then attach an inline planer board to the line. I then let out an additional 100 feet of line. My line-counter reel will then read 125 feet (25 plus 100 equals 125). Once that planer board and lure are in place and fishing, I put the rod in the forward-most of my rod holders, meaning one of the two rod holders nearest the bow of the boat. I then proceed to do the same thing with a second rod, placing it in the forward-most rod holder on the opposite side of the boat. Once that is accomplished, I now have two rods fishing, one on each side of the boat, with both lures running a few feet below the surface. Both those lures are 125 feet behind the boat.

I want the lures on my next two rods running slightly deeper than the first two, so I'll let out 50 feet of line instead of 25. I then clip on an inline planer board and let line out an additional 50 feet, for a total of 100 (50 plus 50 equals 100). I then place that rod in one of the rear-most rod holders, toward the stern of the boat. I repeat that process with my fourth and final rod on the opposite side of the boat.

When I've completed setting up my four-rod trolling spread, I have two lures running a few feet below the surface and two lures running about midway down in the water column. My two "outside" lines are 125 feet back (25 plus 100 equals 125), those lures running higher in the water column. My two "inside" lines are 100 feet back (50 plus 50 equals 100), those lures running about midway down in the water column.

The next step is to adjust the speed of the boat. The slowest my boat's motor (115 horsepower Yamaha four-stroke) will run is about 2.5 miles per hour, which is much too fast for early-spring walleye trolling. To slow the boat to one mile per hour or less, I have to attach two trolling bags, one from the front gunnel on each side of the boat. As an alternative, slowing a boat to trolling speed can also be accomplished by using an electric trolling motor or small, gas-powered outboard, also known as a "kicker." You'll know you've achieved the desired trolling speed by referring to your GPS unit's readout.

Compared to most other species of game fish, walleyes aren't great fighters, and they fight even less in cold water. Nevertheless, it's always a thrill to see an inline planer board start wobbling in the water and then slowly begin moving behind the boat, signaling the first walleye of the season. Another great thing about cold-water, early-spring walleye trolling, especially on Lake Erie, is that if you hook a fish it will most likely be a walleye. There are very few non-target species—walleye anglers call them "junk fish"—active in cold water. But believe me, the non-target species will become more than active later in the year as the water warms, so enjoy this early-spring fishing while it lasts.

One last tip about early-spring walleye trolling also applies to trolling during all seasons of the year. To entice a bite, steer the boat in slow, wide S-turns as you move forward. Doing so causes the lures on the outside of the turn to speed up and the lures on the inside to slow down

These two North Dakota walleye anglers are attempting to coax a bite from reluctant walleyes by using a bow-mounted electric trolling motor to make slow, wide S-turns in the Missouri River near Bismarck.

or even completely stop for a few seconds. This erratic lure action often triggers a strike when simply trolling straight ahead will not.

Making S-turns also helps tell you if the walleyes want a faster or slower lure presentation. For instance, if walleyes are hitting your outside lures on a turn, you may want to increase your trolling speed slightly. If fish are hitting your inside lines during turns, you may want to decrease your speed. Trolling speed is often critical in walleye fishing, especially during early spring, so if you're not getting bit, experiment. Just remember to make very subtle speed adjustments, and less is usually better than more.

Anglers new to walleye trolling often ask whether or not to stop the boat to land a fish. The simple answer is no, don't stop. When a fish hits, continue trolling forward as you normally would and fight the fish to the boat. If it's a particularly large fish, you may want to take the boat out of gear for just a few seconds to let you get the walleye started toward the boat, but this situation is rare. In general, continuing to move the boat forward as you fight and net a fish keeps your other trolling lines in place, untangled, and fishing properly.

Mid to Late-Spring: Trolling Night Crawler Harnesses

Once the surface water temperature reaches about 50 degrees in spring, trolling night crawler harnesses for walleyes becomes productive. This technique is similar in many ways to trolling the large stickbaits just described, but your speed should increase slightly, usually to about 1.5 miles per hour, and possibly to as much as 1.8 to 2.0 miles per hour later in the spring.

I stagger night crawler harnesses throughout the water column, top to bottom, using inline weights. Snap weights can also be used to accomplish this, but inlines won't come off the line inadvertently as snap weights sometimes do.

A good rule of thumb to follow when deciding how far back to place a night crawler harness behind an inline planer board is to consider the depth of water you'll be fishing. For example, if I'm fishing in 30 feet of water, I'll set all my night crawler harnesses back 30 feet behind inline planer boards. I then control the depth at which individual night crawler harnesses run by using one-, two-, and three-ounce inline weights. Here's my typical, beginning trolling spread on any particular fishing day.

If there are three anglers onboard, we can legally fish a total of six rods, two each by Ohio law. I'll place the first two lines, each with a

When netting a walleye while trolling, don't stop the boat. Continuing forward allows your other trolling lines to continue fishing properly and not become entangled with one another.

one-ounce inline weight, 30 feet back, then clip an inline planer board to each of the lines. I then let out an additional 150 feet of line, for a total of 180 feet (30 plus 150 equals 180). I put these two rods in the two rod holders nearest the bow of the boat, one on each side of the boat. Since these first two night crawler harnesses each have a one-ounce inline weight about five feet in front of them, are set 30 feet back behind inline planer boards, and the boat is moving about 1.5 miles per hour, the night crawler harnesses will run about one-third of the way down in a 30-foot water column.

Next, I'll take the two rods with two-ounce weights, set the night crawler harnesses back 30 feet, and clip on inline planer boards. I'll then let out an additional 100 feet of line, for a total of 130 feet (30 plus 100 equals 130). These two rods will then be placed in the middle two rod holders, again, one on each side of the boat. Having two-ounce weights attached to these two lines, these night crawler harnesses will run about half to two-thirds of the way down in a 30-foot water column.

Finally, I'll take my last two rods, each containing three-ounce inline weights, again let out 30 feet of line, and clip on inline planer boards. I then let out an additional 50 feet of line, for a total of 80 feet (30 plus 50 equals 80). In 30 feet of water, these last two night crawler harnesses will run somewhere near the bottom. In essence, I'm straining the water column, top to bottom, by keeping all my lead lengths the same (30 feet), but varying the depth at which the individual night crawler harnesses run by varying the weight of the inline weights.

By using this technique, I've created a V-shaped trolling spread in the water behind the boat. The lightest, one-ounce weights, are running near the top of the V, the two-ounce weights are running somewhere near the middle, and the three-ounce weights are near the point. Hook a fish on any of the outside lines (those lines containing one- or two-ounce weights), and the walleye will pass over the inside line(s) when being reeled in because the inside line(s) are running deeper and the total amount of line out is shorter. Just make sure to allow about 50 feet of spacing between your lines when first setting them out, as already described. Also, when a fish hits, allow a few seconds for the planer board on the line holding the fish to move behind the boat before reeling. If this explanation is as clear as near-shore water after a three-day nor'easter, study the diagram of a basic walleye trolling spread on page 41 and the description should become more understandable.

You can create this same V-shaped configuration in your trolling spread by using the same size inline weight on each line and varying the amount of line you let out. In other words, you could put one-ounce weights on all six rods and stagger them top to bottom in the water column by giving the two outside lines 30 feet of lead, the two middle lines 60 feet of lead, and the two inside lines 90 feet of lead. I prefer using various size inline weights rather than lengthening leads, because it reduces the amount of line out and the amount of reeling necessary when landing a fish or checking a bait.

And speaking of checking baits, trolling night crawler harnesses for walleyes can be very productive, but one downside to this fishing technique is that a crawler can be pulled off a harness by a small fish and you won't always know it's gone. As a result, you may be trolling with no bait on that particular harness, rendering it ineffective. A tip here is to check your night crawler harnesses often while trolling—at least once every 20 minutes or so—making sure the worm is still hooked securely on each hook of the harness. An alternative is to use artificial night crawlers. Berkley Gulp! artificial night crawlers are a good choice, as they have plenty of scent to attract walleyes, and are nearly impossible for fish to pull off the hooks.

Summertime, and the Fishin' Is Easy: Trolling Spoons and Crankbaits

Okay, I'll be honest, walleye fishing is seldom easy, but summer is usually as easy as it gets. Per-hour catch rates for the year peak on most waters during June and July for two reasons. First, as the water warms from spring into summer, walleye metabolism ramps up, literally turning these fish into eating machines. Often during early summer, walleyes are gorging themselves nearly 24 hours per day. Second, there is not as much food in the water during early summer as there will be later in the year when other fish species begin hatching by the gazillions. Simply put, walleyes are *hungry* during early summer and anglers are not competing with millions of baitfish for a walleye's attention.

That said, summer is my favorite time of year to fish for walleyes. Not only are summer days on the Great Lakes and other North American waters extremely pleasant—and usually accompanied by light winds—but the catching is often very good, some days even fantastic! My favorite way to fish for summertime walleyes is to troll spoons. Why? Because it's a relatively easy fishing technique. And to take those spoons to depth, where the walleyes are, I use a combination of Luhr Jensen Jet Divers and Luhr Jensen Dipsy Divers. (See Chapter Three for an in-depth description of these diving planers and how they operate.) Other types of similar diving devices, such as Walker Divers, are also on the market.

Spoons are high-action walleye baits better fished fast than slow: two to three miles per hour. In addition, with your boat moving that quickly you'll be covering about twice the distance per hour than when trolling large stickbaits or night crawler harnesses in spring. As a result, you are likely to encounter more walleyes simply because you'll be covering more water.

A second summertime lure that can be fished in conjunction with spoons are high-action crankbaits. Examples of these types of lures include banana-shaped Reef Runner Deep Divers and Rapala Deep Tail Dancers. Following is a description of the basic trolling spread I use when fishing spoons and crankbaits in tandem, letting the walleyes tell me what lures they like on a particular day. Keep in mind that you could also troll either all spoons or all crankbaits, but for illustration purposes I'll be describing how to run both spoons and high-action crankbaits at the same time.

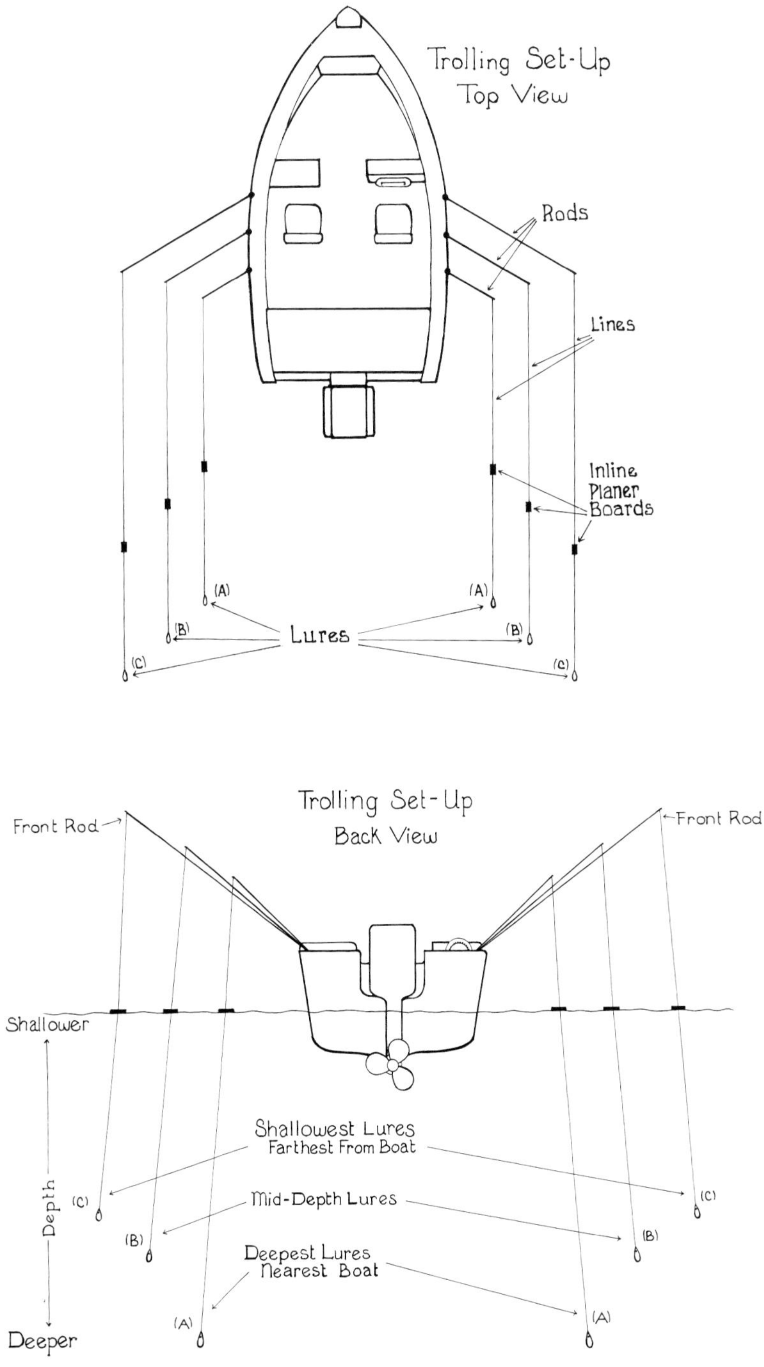

A typical walleye trolling spread viewed both from above and behind a boat.

If I have two other anglers aboard in addition to myself, we'll be fishing a total of six rods with three of the lines pulling spoons and three trailing crankbaits. I usually run all the spoons on one side of the boat and all the crankbaits on the other. I'm sure the lures could be intermixed without causing too many problems, but I like to standardize and simplify my trolling techniques as much as possible. Create too many variables and things can quickly become chaotic, especially if something happens to go wrong while on the water. By having all my spoons fishing on one side of the boat and all my crankbaits on the other, I don't have to think too hard, and that's a good thing. For instance, if I catch a fish on a spoon, I know that spoon goes back in the water on the left side of the boat. And if I catch a fish on a crankbait, I know that lure goes back into the water on the right side of the boat. I like things simple, and this system seems to work well for me.

Let's begin by setting the spoon side of the boat first. At the start of the day, I'll choose three different colors of spoons, making sure one of them is gold, hammered on the front to reflect more light. Gold is my favorite Lake Erie spoon color, especially in clear water, and I give it the best place in the trolling spread. Year in and year out, that spot seems to be the farthest outside trolling line.

I don't know what it is about that particular location in the trolling spread, but when fishing spoons, the outside lures seem to get hit more often than the others. It may be that those spoons are the ones farthest from the boat and that making S-turns imparts more action and/or speed to those particular lures. Like I said, I don't know what it is for sure, but when trolling spoons I put my best color, usually solid gold, on an outside line, and take it down to depth with a Jet Diver.

To get the spoon to the desired depth, say halfway down in 30 feet of water, I let out 50 feet of line. I then clip an inline planer board onto the line and set the rod in one of the forward-most rod holders. Push the alarm clicker button of your line-counter reel to the "on" position, and it will put just enough tension on the line to allow the line and planer board to play out without the reel back-lashing. Once the line-counter reel reaches the total amount of line out you desire, throw the free-spool lever to engage the reel spool and you're fishing. This first spoon I set 150 feet from the boat. So if I first let out 50 feet of line before snapping on an inline planer board, I then let out an additional 100 feet of line. The total on that line-counter reel will read 150 (50 plus 100 equals 150).

My second lure on the spoon side of the boat will be set back a little farther than the first, say 75 feet rather than 50. That will make the spoon run a little deeper, about two-thirds of the way down in 30 feet of water behind a size #40 Jet Diver. I then clip on an inline planer board and place that rod in the middle rod holder. Letting out an additional 50 feet of line, that line-counter reel will read 125 (75 plus 50 equals 125).

My third and final spoon I'll place behind a Dipsy Diver, either size 0 or size 1. Note that I don't put an inline planer board on this line. This rod goes into the rod holder closest to the stern of the boat. I let out enough line so that the Dipsy Diver takes the spoon down and is fishing just a few feet off the bottom. Again, as described when fishing inline weights and night crawler harnesses, I'm creating a V-shaped trolling spread. The highest spoon is running on the outside of the spread, about halfway down, and closest to the top of the V; the middle spoon is running about two-thirds of the way down in the water column, close to the middle of the V; and the deepest spoon, the one behind the Dipsy Diver, is closest to the point of the V. Thus far, I've completed one side of my trolling spread using spoons. I'll use crankbaits to complete the other side.

In choosing crankbaits for summertime trolling, I want a lure with a large lip so that it will dive to the desired depth without having to put any weight or diving device in front of it. That said, I like Reef Runner Deep Divers and Rapala Deep Tail Dancers. In fact, my first 10-pound walleye was caught by trolling a Rapala Deep Tail Dancer (size 11), the specific color being purple clown flash. An additional classic high-action, large-lipped crankbait that has caught millions of walleyes from Lake Erie and other bodies of water during summer is the Hot 'N Tot.

If fishing about 30 feet of water, my first lure on the crankbait side of the trolling spread will be set back 50 feet. I'll then attach an inline planer board to the line. Letting out an additional 100 feet of line, the line-counter reel will read 150 (50 plus 100 equals 150). I then place that rod in the forward-most rod holder. The next crankbait will be set back a little farther, say 75 feet, which will cause it to run deeper than the first. An inline planer board is attached and an additional 50 feet of line let out. The line-counter will read 125 when the lure is in place (75 plus 50 equals 125), and that rod will be placed in the middle rod holder.

The third and final lure on the crankbait side of the trolling spread I'll put behind a Dipsy Diver. But this lure will not be a large-lipped crankbait like the other two. If it is, the large lip on the bait will counteract the diving ability of the Dipsy Diver, trying to pull the rear of the diving device down. When running a crankbait behind a Dipsy Diver, choose a crank with a short bill or even no bill at all, and allow the Dipsy Diver to take the lure to depth. A good choice for a bait of this type is a Reef Runner Ripstick or Rapala Original Floating Minnow, as those models of lures have only a small diving bill. This third and final rod on the crankbait side of the boat will be placed in the rod holder nearest the stern.

Remember, the trolling spread just described—spoons and crankbaits—is a summer, warm-water trolling setup, the time of year when most walleyes are usually found lower in the water column, anywhere from about mid-depths to near the bottom. But that said, don't be afraid to run at least one lure high from time to time. Often, especially at dawn and dusk, walleyes can be found very high in the water column, sometimes feeding just a few feet below the surface. You won't see those high fish on your sonar screen because they will scatter to the side of the boat as you approach. But running a spoon or crankbait near the surface behind an inline planer board, out to the side of your boat, will tell you whether or not those fish are there.

Fall Fishing

As the hardwood forests surrounding the Great Lakes and across North America gradually take on their annual, brilliant autumn colors, some of the best walleye fishing of the year is yet to be enjoyed. Crisp fall days spent on the water are invigorating, and cloudless blue skies provide the perfect backdrop for a day of walleye trolling. But beware the fall storms. The winds of change are blowing this time of year, cold winds that will bring ice to the lakes in a few short months, ending walleye trolling for the year. So make the most of these fleeting, idyllic days of fall. They won't last long.

That said, fall walleye trolling is a mirror image of spring fishing. As the water cools during September, October, and November, the high-speed tactics and high-action baits of summer give way to more subtle lure and bait presentations. This is the time of year to once again begin slowing down your fishing techniques. I go back to pulling night crawler harnesses behind inline weights or using moderate-action crankbaits, and just before ice-up I return to trolling large stickbaits pulled very slowly—one mile per hour or less—just like during early

Fall fishing for walleyes is similar to trolling for them in the spring of the year, only in reverse. As the water gradually cools in fall, slow down your trolling presentations as you would in spring, and increase the size of your lures.

spring. And as in spring, some of the largest walleyes of the year are caught during fall. In fact, it's the season of year when I caught my first 10-pounder.

So there you have it, my basic walleye trolling spreads spring through fall. But if you're not getting a bite on any particular day, don't be afraid to experiment. Who knows, I've seen days on the water when spring and fall tactics worked well in the heat of summer and vice versa. Just because a specific trolling technique is *supposed* to work during a certain time of year doesn't mean it will. And when those days occur—and they will—possibly a combination of approaches is what you'll need to put fish in the boat. The point is to not get locked into just one trolling technique or method. Learn to be versatile in your approach to trolling, and you'll catch more walleyes. For example, the following is a summer technique used by long-time Wisconsin professional walleye angler Keith Kavajecz when things aren't going so well.

Suspended Summer Walleyes: What to Do When the Fishing Gets Tough

Kavajecz's number-one lure choice for trolling suspended summer walleyes is a crankbait. Because the water's warmest at that time of year and the fish are aggressive, he usually wants a bait with a lot of action. But if fishing conditions suddenly get tough because of a summer cold front, wind, or both, he'll revert to a live-bait presentation he usually uses when trolling during spring and fall: night crawler harnesses.

"Anytime you're fishing for suspended walleyes, whether with crankbaits or night crawler harnesses, you want to run your baits above the fish you're marking," Kavajecz said. "What I'm trying to do when I begin fishing on any particular day is first find fish with my electronics, then find the feeding zone of those fish. And that may not be at the same depth I'm marking them on my graph—usually it's higher. What walleyes typically do when they suspend in open water is to hold at one level, but rise up and feed on baitfish that swim over them at a higher level. My job is to find that feeding zone."

Kavajecz searches for this feeding zone during a tough bite with night crawler harnesses weighted with inline weights. To probe the depths, he either varies the length of line he lets out before attaching an inline planer board, or varies the size of the inline weight itself. For example, he may run a two-ounce inline weight on all of his lines, but let out different lengths of line behind the planer boards—10 feet, 20 feet, 30 feet, etc. Or, he may make all the line lengths the same, but vary the size of the inline weight, running a one-ounce weight on one line, a two-ounce on another, and a three-ounce on a third. The possible line-length and weight combinations are many, and he continues to experiment until he begins catching fish. Once he's fine-tuned his presentation, he sets up other trolling lines in a similar fashion.

"My fishing partner [fellow walleye pro Gary Parsons] and I first got the idea for the type of inline weights we now fish with from a friend on Lake Huron's Saginaw Bay," Kavajecz said. "He was tying a flutter spoon between his inline weights and night crawler harnesses to give the presentation more flash. That gave us the idea to try putting colored prism tape on the inline weights ahead of our own open-water crawler harnesses and eliminate the flutter spoon. The set-up worked so well for walleyes that we went to Bass Pro Shops with the idea and they eventually developed the Fish Weight. Available in one-, two-, and three-ounce sizes, the bodies are fish-shaped and holographic in color."

Precision Trolling Pro

How deep do various crankbaits run? A tool that makes the accurate placement of these lures in the water column simple is the manual *Precision Trolling Pro*. “The preliminary pages are an in-depth study of trolling techniques, followed by life-size color pictures of crankbaits,” said author Mark Romanack. “Each page also contains a dive curve for the bait listed, showing graphically how much line to let out, in feet, to achieve certain trolling depths.” Available online at www.fishing411.net, *Precision Trolling Pro* is listed at $29.95, and, yeah, it’s worth the price. Individual dive cures for specific lures may also be purchased through your smart phone.

Behind the inline weights Kavajecz attaches his spinner–night crawler harness combination. He ties his own by beginning with a fluorocarbon leader (14- to 17-pound test), cut to four feet. To the end of the leader he ties a #4 Mustad Triple-Grip treble hook, and above that a single #1 red-colored hook, Mustad’s Double Wide. He believes that just a touch of red may convince a wary walleye that what it is considering eating is already injured and may be an easy meal. Kavajecz next adds a few colored beads or a spacer body. The advantage of a spacer body is that it spins slowly on the line when pulled through water, giving off added flash and vibration. Above the spacer or beads he slides on a quick-change clevis and adds a #5, #6, or #7 Indiana or Colorado spinner blade to complete the rig, again in a holographic color.

“I fish these open-water night crawler harnesses slowly,” Kavajecz said, “as slow as 0.5 and normally slower than one mile per hour, as opposed to crankbaits, which are trolled about 1.8 miles per hour, but can be pulled as fast as three miles per hour. Crankbaits let you cover more water faster, but if the fish don’t want cranks on a particular day, I suggest trying a spinner with a worm. Use either a whole, natural night crawler or an artificial crawler with scent. Night crawler harnesses are more of a slow-it-down, in-your-face presentation that just may entice walleyes during a tough bite.”

A final tip from Keith Kavajecz is for anglers who have depth finders powerful enough to detect a thermocline when one exists: “The more active fish will usually be above the thermocline, and the less active fish usually below it,” he said. “If you can run your baits within five or 10 feet of the thermocline, you’ll catch more walleyes.”

Chapter 5

Choices, Choices

Choosing Crankbaits for Walleye Trolling

The Great Lakes are well-suited for trolling crankbaits, as the vast, open water of the "Five Sisters" provides untold numbers of suspended baitfish. Consequently, walleyes lurk below these bait balls, and pulling minnow or shad-imitation crankbaits through these schools of hungry fish can quickly fill a livewell.

But with the confusing array of shapes, sizes, and colors of crankbaits on the market today, how do you know which lure is best and when to use it? To keep things simple, think of crankbaits as specific tools in your tackle box to be deployed at different times of the year and at different depths. By learning how to select the appropriate crank for the appropriate season and water temperature, you'll catch more walleyes more consistently. Bigger fish, too.

"One of the best ways to catch a really big walleye, especially if you're a novice troller, is to learn how to crankbait fish," said professional walleye angler Keith Kavajecz of Kaukauna, Wisconsin. "I've probably caught more big fish—eight pounds plus—using crankbaits than all of my other fishing techniques combined."

But according to Kavajecz, not all crankbaits are created equal. He says that a good walleye crankbait must have a roll to it. "Watch the bait's eyes as it moves through the water. If the eyes don't move up and down, put the bait in your bass tackle box. Every crankbait I've ever used that consistently catches walleyes has a rolling, top-to-bottom movement to it."

Good Vibrations

Kavajecz believes that the first thing to draw a walleye to any type of bait is vibration and sound, with shape and color being secondary. Every crankbait produces a vibration while moving through the water, but Keith says that even the very same make and model of lure will generate slightly different vibrations. This is most noticeable during tough bites, when fish are not aggressive.

"For example," he said, "you might be trolling four rods, all with the same baits, but one lure catches more fish than the others. You can even change sides of the boat with that lure, and it still catches more fish. The reason is because that particular crankbait has just the right

Another nice walleye comes to the net. Learn to troll crankbaits, and you'll be netting more walleyes more often. Think of crankbaits as individual tools in a toolbox, to be used at specific depths and specific times of the year.

Long-time Wisconsin pro angler Keith Kavajecz has a walleye netted for him by his amateur partner for the day during a tournament on Lake Huron's Saginaw Bay.

vibration the fish want on that particular day. That's why if you're not catching fish, constant experimenting with various crankbaits is so important. My advice is to keep changing bait styles until you find something that works."

Subtle-Action Crankbaits

Early in the year, when water temperatures are below 45 degrees, Kavajecz prefers crankbaits with a subtle action. Usually these are stickbaits with a small diving bill and a long, thin body. Examples include the Rapala Original Floating Minnow, sizes 9 to 13 (Keith prefers the old-style balsa, not plastic); Reef Runner Ripsticks; and Smithwick Rattlin' Rogues.

Deep-diving versions of these baits set the all-time, single-tournament catch record on the now defunct Professional Walleye Trail (PWT) tournament circuit in 2002. Held on Lake Erie in April, three days of perfect weather saw 346 post-spawn walleyes in excess of 10 pounds come to the scales. Ted Takasaki also set a one-day PWT record of five walleyes that weighed 53.20 pounds. The total weight record was set by tournament winner Tommy Skarlis—15 fish that weighed an incredible 138.28 pounds! All told, every fifth fish of the tournament was in excess of 10 pounds, and the tournament average for all walleyes weighed was 7.9 pounds.

"Many of the big fish in that tournament were caught on Rapala Deep Husky Jerks and other subtle- to moderate-action crankbaits fished 50 feet or so behind inline planer boards," Kavajecz said. "We were running those baits in about 30 feet of water and they were diving to only about eight feet, so the fish were fairly high in the water column."

Moderate- and High-Action Crankbaits

As the water warms to 50 degrees and above, crankbaits with moderate actions seem to catch more walleyes. In general, these baits have larger diving bills, more flash, and more vibration than the subtle-action baits. If money is a consideration and you have to choose just one style of crankbait for year-round use, these would be it. Keith Kavajecz's choices for moderate-action crankbaits include Berkley Flicker Shads, Storm Deep Jr. Thunder Sticks, and Rapala Husky Jerks.

When summer is in full swing and water temperatures are at their highest for the year, high-action crankbaits for aggressive walleyes

This walleye hit a Deep Jr. Thunder Stick crankbait. The lure is attached to the line with a snap not a snap-swivel. A snap-swivel is slightly heavier than a snap and will deaden some of the lure's action.

are a good choice. "The classic example of this type of bait is the Hot 'N Tot," Keith said, "because it has a good roll, as well as a wide wobble. Another high-action bait I like real well in summer is the Reef Runner. By letting out 350 feet of 10/4 FireLine, I can get it to dive as much as 40 feet. I also like the larger-size Berkley Flicker Shads in warm water. The #7 and #9 Flicker Shads have a more aggressive action that calls fish from farther distances."

Another of Kavajecz's secrets is to troll jointed crankbaits during summer. He's found that the wagging tail section of these baits gives off a lot of vibration. "One of my favorite lures of all time is a jointed, shad-style bait. Why? Because I once won $100,000 on such a bait during a tournament," he grinned.

Crankbait Colors

As for what colors to select for walleye crankbaits, Kavajecz suggests keeping things simple. "As a general rule, in clear water I'll use more natural colors such as blues, blacks, silvers, and Tennessee shad. My favorite color in clear water is rainbow trout. In dingy water, I'll go with brighter colors such as Firetiger, which has green, chartreuse,

In relatively clear water, gold is always a good choice for a walleye crankbait, such as this Reef Runner Ripstick. When choosing crankbaits, first decide how deep you want a particular bait to run, then consider vibration, color, and size of the lure.

Run Silent, Run Deep

Jim Cooper of Lorain, Ohio, is a retired charter captain who regularly fishes crankbaits in Lake Erie's Central Basin. Mainly a troller, Cooper runs as many as 16 lines at a time, employing a combination of large planer boards on a mast system, diving devices, and downriggers to get his lines down and out.

"One thing I do differently at times with crankbaits is to troll them deep in muddy water," Cooper said. "It's always best to fish clear water whenever possible, but after a big storm on Erie it's often impossible to find clean water. On those days, running a Reef Runner or Bomber Long A deep off the board lines will sometimes produce fish. I'm not sure why it works, it just does."

and orange in it. Studies have shown that chartreuse and orange are the two colors walleyes see best.

"But my all-time favorite color," Kavajecz continued, "the one I put on first when trying to figure out what color is best that day, is pearl white. Gary Parsons and I call it 'mouse.' It's basically a white lure with a gray top. White is a great all-around color for walleyes, as it looks natural but also stands out well in stained waters."

Ultimately, Kavajecz lets the fish decide what colors they want, occasionally having to break his own rules. "I remember fishing Lake Michigan's Bay-de-Noc in the Upper Peninsula a few years back, in very clear water, and for some reason that day the walleyes wanted their crankbaits all red. Not just a touch of red mind you, but all red, so that's what I gave them."

One of Keith's favorite colors for open-water trolling is "clown" because of the touch of red in the paint pattern. He believes that red may make a bait look injured, signaling an easy meal for a hungry walleye. Sometimes he'll even add a touch of red paint to a crankbait while on the water.

Most of the walleye crankbaits mentioned by Keith Kavajecz have been around for years and have proven themselves fish catchers season after season. Other baits he did not name, such as Bomber Long As and Cotton Cordell Wally Divers, have also been staples of serious walleye anglers for decades.

When crankbait trolling, it's important to have a good selection of actions, sizes, and colors of lures. Some trollers also tip their crankbaits with a small piece of night crawler to add an enticing scent for walleyes.

Reef Runners

A crankbait that has wobbled its way into the walleye world within the past two decades is the Reef Runner. These banana-shaped crankbaits—developed by Scott Stecher of Marblehead, Ohio, on the south shore of Lake Erie—have proven themselves consistent walleye getters on waters across North America. The baits are known specifically as Ripsticks (both shallow divers and deep divers), Little Rippers, and Ripshads. Stecher's company also produces the popular Cicada walleye blade bait.

Stecher considers his crankbaits high-action, which he says allows them to be trolled on lead-core line or behind inline weights or drop weights and still retain much of what he terms the baits' unique "hunting" characteristics. "The baits kick out to the side erratically when trolled or retrieved after a cast," Stecher said. "This searching action of the crankbait is what often triggers a strike from walleyes."

He also believes that his baits are so productive because of the total spectrum of colors he offers. "My best-selling colors of Reef Runner crankbaits are Bare Naked, Pink Lemonade, Firetiger, and Eriedescent," Stecher said, "but I'm always experimenting with new color combinations."

The names of some of Stecher's existing colors are hilarious: Fried Chicken, Cheap Sunglasses, Trailer Trash, Dr. Dreadful, and the ever-popular Monkey Puke.

Size Matters

After deciding which crankbait action and color to use, the size of the lure should be your next consideration. Pro walleye angler Mark Brumbaugh likes a large crankbait in spring, "because the size of prey is larger at that time of year," he reasons. Larry Lambert, a charter captain on Lake Erie's Western Basin, agrees. "Keep in mind that walleyes, especially big fish just coming off the spawn, want a meal, not a snack," Lambert said.

During summer, some anglers switch to smaller-sized crankbaits, believing those lures better match the size of the majority of baitfish at that time of year. As already mentioned, one of Keith Kavajecz's secrets is to troll jointed crankbaits in summer. He's found that the wagging tail section of these baits produces lots of vibration, attracting reluctant walleyes. Still other anglers stay with a larger bait, believing it better stands out from fry and fingerlings, making it easier to see. Just as each angler is different, each day on the water is different. During summer, a good rule of thumb is to run various-sized crankbaits, letting the fish tell you what they prefer.

A Smithwick Rattlin' Rogue stickbait caught this walleye. Notice the lure's orange belly and large diving bill.

A Few More Tips on Choosing Crankbaits

As for choosing colors of crankbaits, Mark Brumbaugh and many other walleye pros usually use more natural colors in clearer water (chrome/ black, perch, etc.) and more unnatural colors in stained or muddy water (chartreuse, Firetiger, etc.). "White-colored crankbaits can often be good, too, because of the many alewives and shad in the Great Lakes" said Brumbaugh. "And another great color on all the lakes is purple." A final tip from Brumbaugh is to make sure all your crankbaits are properly tuned—running straight and true—and that hooks are "sticky-sharp."

Trolling Lines for Crankbaits

Yet another decision concerning crankbaits is what line to troll them on, mono or braid. Mark Brumbaugh prefers 10-pound Trilene XT in cold water, believing it hooks more fish than braid at that time of year because of the mono's stretch. But he will use a braided superline in summer to get baits deeper. Keith Kavajecz also likes braid for getting baits deep. "By letting out 350 feet of 10/4 FireLine, I can get some crankbaits to dive as much as 40 feet on their own with no added weight," he said.

Speed Kills

How fast to troll crankbaits? Mark Brumbaugh usually begins at about one mile per hour in cold water, bumping it up to two or nearly three miles per hour in warm water. But he says that more often than not it's the change in direction of a crankbait rather than speed that triggers a bite. "With walleyes, on many days it's a reaction bite," he said. "Speed up, slow down, stop, change direction; it all makes a crankbait move erratically. You just have to experiment."

Search and Destroy

Mark Brumbaugh, Keith Kavajecz, and other professional walleye anglers do a lot of searching for open-water walleyes with their electronics before ever putting a crankbait or other lure in the water. "Some of the newer sonar units allow you to run just up on plane at

20 to 25 miles per hour and still graph fish," Kavajecz said. "If you don't have a sonar unit that will do that, I suggest running for half a mile and then slowing down to watch your graph for 100 yards or so. If you don't see anything, keep repeating this process until you find what you think are walleyes or bait fish. This may at first seem like unproductive time because you are not actually 'fishing,' but believe me it is well worth the effort on the Great Lakes, where there are large open basins with little if any structure—and often no walleyes."

As the seasons change and water cools, autumn crankbait fishing becomes a mirror image of spring. When water temperatures begin to drop, crankbait actions should change from high, to moderate, and finally, once again, back to subtle. Trolling speeds should slow, too. And if you've been pulling smaller crankbaits in summer, gradually increase their size as fall progresses.

Fishing crankbaits is only one of many productive trolling techniques for catching walleyes from big water. It's a relatively simple technique, but not one that's easily mastered. To those unfamiliar with pulling cranks, it may even appear as the ultimate "no-brainer" in walleye fishing—just clip on a bait, throw it over the side of the boat, and put the motor in gear. But to those anglers aware of the subtleties, crankbait trolling is a technique requiring attention to detail and constant tweaking. Learn to be a better crankbait troller and . . . wait a minute, there's a fish, get the net!

How to Tune a Crankbait

If a crankbait is not well "tuned" it's not fishing properly, and likely not catching fish. When trolled, a crankbait should run in a straight line. If the bait pulls to the left or right behind your boat, tuning the lure is required.

Some crankbaits are designed to erratically kick out to the side a foot or two when trolled—producing what's known as a "hunting action"—but a properly tuned crankbait will quickly return to the centerline. If it doesn't, here's how to tune it.

Take a pair of needle-nose pliers and bend the metal eyelet of the crankbait (where you attach the snap or snap-swivel) to the left or right, but only slightly. Make the bend in the opposite direction the lure is tracking. For example, if the lure is tracking to the left, bend the ring to the right. If the lure is tracking to the right, bend the ring to the left. But do so in small increments, as even a small bend will go a long way in altering the track of the bait.

After making each adjustment, put the lure back in the water and troll it behind the boat 10 or 20 feet to see if it's running true. If not, keep tweaking until the crankbait is fishing properly. Reef Runner makes a small, inexpensive tool for tuning its crankbaits called a Tune-a-Fish, which makes this job much easier. If you fish Reef Runner crankbaits, get one.

To "tune" a crankbait to make it run properly, use a pair of needle-nose pliers and bend the attachment eyelet (not the split ring) on the lip of the lure to the left or right, opposite of the direction the lure is running. Make only slight adjustments, as a little tweaking goes a long way.

Chapter 6

Going Walleye Trolling

Determining When and Where

The Great Lakes and other large bodies of water in North America containing walleyes are vast areas. Millions of walleyes live in these waters, but there are also millions of square acres containing no walleyes. It's your job as an angler to figure out where the fish are before starting to troll for them. And in doing so, it's better to use a rifle-type approach rather than a shotgun approach. In other words, you want to be as exact as possible about where you plan to fish *before* leaving the dock. If you don't, you could spend many unproductive hours trolling unproductive water. It's also a good idea to have a "Plan B" in mind, should things not go as hoped at your primary location. Here's how to prepare for a day of fishing.

Being a freelance outdoors writer, I have the luxury of fishing whenever I want to. I can usually adjust my work schedule to take advantage of the best weather and reports of a hot bite. I realize most anglers don't have that option, and must go fishing when they can. If that's your situation, by all means go fishing when the opportunity presents itself. Don't sit home and wait for ideal conditions, because they may never arrive. But if you can have your "druthers" as to when to fish, here's what to look for.

Watch the Weather

As an outdoorsman I'm constantly watching the weather, but when I'm planning a potential fishing trip my interest in the local forecast increases considerably. A week to five days or so before a potential trip, I begin watching local television long-range weather forecasts. What I'm looking for is the prediction of a two- to three-day warm front with increasing or at least stable temperatures each day. In planning that far in advance, I also keep in mind that the predicted warm- or stable-weather front may stall and arrive a day or two late or pick up speed and arrive a day or two early. In general, though, I know the day I'm targeting to fish, give or take a day either way.

Go Online

My next step is to go online to several favorite walleye fishing Web sites I have bookmarked on my computer. Walleye Central (www.walleyecentral.com) is an excellent site, containing up-to-date walleye catch information from around the country. While on this and other local Web sites, I check out the latest catch reports for the lake and area I plan to fish. I primarily fish Lake Erie's Western and Central basins, so I search for specific catch reports from those two areas. What I'm looking for is current information about not only *if* walleyes are being caught, but *where* and *how* are they being caught. How deep are the fish? What baits/lures/presentations are working best? How fast are anglers trolling? Is it a morning, evening, or night bite? Those kinds of questions are all important.

Everyone Needs Friends

Once I've reviewed the latest general, online catch reports—is the bite hot or not?—I begin to get more specific by contacting my individual fishermen friends, guys I trust to provide me not only with accurate fishing information but also with what is called MRI, Most Recent Information. MRI is critical to getting you on fish quickly once you're actually on the water. Walleyes can travel miles in a day on big water, and where they were several days ago, or maybe even yesterday or today, may not be where they will be tomorrow.

It took me years to figure this out, but I eventually learned the hard way that if I developed a network of credible contacts who are on the water daily, and who were willing to share their fishing information with me, I would become a more successful fisherman because I'd be fishing where the fish are. I have an outdoor-writer friend from Texas who always advises, "Dig where there's 'taters!" What he means is to fish where the fish are. That may sound like a no-brainer, but it's a basic concept overlooked by many fishermen time and again. Don't fish where walleyes were yesterday, last week, last month, or last year at this time, fish where they are now.

Over the years, I've developed relationships with marina operators, charter boat captains, fishery biologists, bait shop owners, walleye

MRI (Most Recent Information) is critical to getting you on walleyes quickly. Develop a network of fishing friends you share information with, and everyone wins.

pros, and other just plain good fishermen who are either on the water daily or are in touch with anglers who are. These guys know where the walleyes are at any particular time and how to catch them. A day or two before my planned fishing trip, I'm burning up my cell phone minutes or emailing these guys asking the "where" and "how" questions: *where* are the walleyes, and *how* are they being caught?

I usually have to trailer my boat anywhere from an hour and a half to two and a half hours to get to Lake Erie from where I live in north-central Ohio, so with the price of gas these days I want to make as few

Bait stores are usually a good source of up-to-date fishing information, but always corroborate what they tell you with other sources of information.

unproductive fishing trips as possible. These valuable, personal contacts with people living along the lakeshore allow me to do just that. If the fishing is good, my contacts tell me so, and are glad to provide specific GPS coordinates, as well. If the fishing is not so hot, they tell me that, too, saving me a less-than-productive trip.

Keep in mind that some bait and tackle shops may not always give you the straight scoop. Most do, but some "gild the lily" at times to get you to make that road trip during times of marginal fishing, hoping you'll stop on your way and spend some money at their store. So take what some bait shop owners say with a grain of salt, and always corroborate what they tell you with other information sources.

Check the Nearshore Marine Forecast

One last thing I do before actually making my fishing trip is to go back online and check the Nearshore Marine Forecast provided by the National Weather Service for the specific day and area I plan to fish. I do this several times the day before fishing and again early in the morning just before leaving the house on the day of the trip. I do so frequently because the forecast may suddenly change at the last minute, especially during spring and fall when weather fronts are more frequent and more severe. The Great Lakes and other large bodies of water are no place to be during storms or high winds. I've found the Nearshore Marine Forecast of wind and wave predictions provided by the National Weather Service to be accurate most of the time, so heed their warnings, especially if a small-craft advisory is predicted. Don't take chances with your safety, or that of your fishing buddies.

The day after my fishing trip I make it a point to tell my fishing friends and contacts how I did and if I learned any new information that might benefit them. MRI is a two-way street, and what goes around comes around. If you're generous with your fishing information, others will return the favor and everyone wins. In short, develop a network of credible fishing contacts and you'll catch more walleyes.

Keep a Fishing Log

Something that will help you find more fish long-term is keeping a written log of all your fishing trips. After each of my days on the water, I take time to record the date, time, location, weather, and specific trolling techniques used (crankbaits, spoons, night crawler harnesses, etc.), as well as the catch. Referring to this log the same time next year helps remind me of where walleyes are likely to be at that time

Cell phones are used as much today as marine radios to keep anglers in touch with one another while on the water and stay on the walleyes. Just remember that you may not get a cell phone signal too far from shore, so always have a backup communication system onboard for safety reasons.

of year, and also what presentations worked in the past and what didn't. And be very specific in recording details in your log, such as lead lengths, colors of lures used, trolling speed, etc. All that information is important because, from year to year, you won't remember as much as you think you will.

But, What If . . .

But what if you're planning to fish a lake that's new to you, possibly somewhere hundreds of miles away where you haven't already established fishing contacts? What do you do then? Start by obtaining a map of the lake and its surroundings, possibly online through a state or provincial Department of Natural Resources or local travel and tourism agency. What you are looking for is a detailed fishing map showing lake depth-contour lines. Studying the map will give you a general idea of where walleyes might be found during the time of year you're planning to fish.

Online fishing Web sites should be your next step in the search for walleye information about a lake new to you. And if you don't find the specific fishing information you seek, ask. Many anglers are willing to share their fishing knowledge, especially if they know you're out of the area. Post an information request on a fishing Web site or two, and you'll likely be pleasantly surprised at the amount of information you quickly receive in return.

Contacting bait and tackle stores in the area you plan to fish is also a good idea, as these establishments are usually dependable sources of basic fishing information. Note that I said usually, but not always. Mention to the owner or employee you talk to over the phone that you're from out of the area, and they will likely be willing to fill you in on where walleyes are in their lake currently and the techniques the locals are using to catch them. In return for this information, stop by the tackle shop when you arrive, introduce yourself, and spend a little money on baits or snacks. I've found that spending some money goes a long way toward saying thanks, especially if you experience good fishing and plan to return in the future.

However, the absolute best way to obtain the most specific, on-the-water fishing information for a lake unfamiliar to you is to hire a professional fishing guide for the first day or half-day of your trip. A reputable guide usually doesn't come cheap, but it will be money well spent, as he can get you on the fish much quicker than you can find them yourself. And as you're fishing with him, you'll be able to pick his brain as to how and where to most productively spend the remainder of your fishing time on the lake. Simply put, hiring a guide will make your following fishing days that much more successful.

Ultimately, knowing when and where to fish on a particular body of water boils down to experience. The more you go fishing, the more you'll know when conditions are right and when they're not. But, again, don't sit home waiting for fishing conditions to be perfect, because they seldom are. Go fishing when you can, and sooner or later the fishing gods will smile upon you, at times when you least expect it.

And one more thing. Go fishing with new people occasionally, especially anglers you believe are better fishermen than you. Everyone does things a little differently, and by fishing with other good anglers you'll pick up a tip or two that will help you on the water. Just don't forget to return the favor when other, possibly less experienced anglers, want to go fishing with you.

Home-Field Disadvantage?

I'm not a tournament walleye fisherman. I never have been and likely never will be. There's just something about someone telling me where and when to fish and then charging me money to do it that rubs me the wrong way.

That said, I have no problem with walleye tournaments in general and walleye tournament fishermen specifically. In fact, there is much to be learned from these guys, especially the full-time walleye pros, and I've found most of them are very forthcoming with their fishing knowledge and information. Okay, at least *after* a tournament is over. But can a walleye angler become too familiar with his home water, to the point where he becomes stuck in a fishing rut and not catching the number of walleyes he could? I posed that question to several professional walleye anglers, and the answers I received were very insightful.

Mark Brumbaugh

A walleye pro since 1991, Mark Brumbaugh of Arcanum, Ohio, believes that when local fishermen on a particular lake don't do well, they are fishing "memories." "We all tend to do it at times, especially if you fish the same places year after year," he said. "The problem with fishing memories is that the fish are always changing location."

Brumbaugh gave an example from a professional walleye tournament held several years ago in Hudson, Wisconsin, during October. "Timing was everything at that tournament," Brumbaugh said. "In rivers, walleyes are constantly moving and changing locations in the

Whether you plan to participate in walleye tournaments or not, there is much to be learned from tournament fishermen, especially the pros, as they are forced to fish in all types of weather conditions. Pictured is a flotilla of pro anglers leaving the dock for another day of tournament fishing.

current, and if you weren't in the right spot at the right time, you didn't catch fish."

The first location Brumbaugh fished on day one of the tournament was an industrial water discharge in Pool Three of the Mississippi River. The spot was known for producing good fish, and he had caught walleyes there during practice. "I went there first thing in the morning, fished an hour and a half, but didn't catch anything so I moved," he said. "I found out later that the winner of the tournament fished there, too, only in the afternoons."

Brumbaugh's advice is to approach your home waters as someone who has never seen the lake or river before. "Search the entire system, just like everyone else is doing," he said. "Use your knowledge of the area, but try to suspend any preconceived ideas of where you think walleyes might be."

Ernie Olson

A well-known walleye guide on Minnesota's Mille Lacs, Ernie Olson has been tournament fishing since 1996 and competing as a pro since 2000. He agrees with Brumbaugh that fishing "memories" can be a hindrance, and that doing so has been his downfall more than once.

"The tournaments I do best in seem to be the ones where I stay on the fish that are most active," he said. "I've found that when I return to the location where I caught my last fish during pre-fishing for a tournament is when I have my greatest success. I then try and force myself to stay on that bite and not go chasing locations where I think walleyes *should* be."

Olson once used that strategy to take second place in the Mille Lacs, Minnesota, Wave Wacker invitational tournament, an annual competition with a first prize of as much as $100,000. Some 200 boats usually enter in any given year, but despite that amount of stiff competition Olson still manages to cash a check more often than not.

He believes that another reason some anglers don't do well at home is that they get intimidated when big-name pro walleye anglers roll into town. "Just knowing the pros are on the water may take some local fishermen off their game a bit," he said.

Another consideration Olson mentioned was the pro-am format used during most walleye tournaments. "If a guy is used to always fishing with his long-time fishing buddy and then he's suddenly forced to fish with a total stranger for three days, that can sometimes

A Fisherman's Poem: Good Advice

Wind from the North,
a fisherman does not go forth.

Wind from the East,
the fish bite least.

Wind from the South,
blows the bait in the fish's mouth.

Wind from the West,
the fish bite best.

This simple, anonymous poem has been around for years, and is good advice when determining, generally, when to go fishing. And not just for walleyes, but most any fish species. The poem's tenets don't always hold true, but usually do, and here's why.

Winds blowing from the North and East bring cold-weather fronts, which tend to turn fish off from feeding, likely due to changes in barometric pressure. You *can* catch fish during cold fronts, but usually you have to slow down your trolling presentation, as well as reduce the size of the bait or lure you use. You also must be more exact in your presentation, in essence dropping the bait or lure on a walleye's nose. Fish are simply not as aggressive nor do they feed as much during a cold front.

South and West winds, on the other hand, usher in warm-weather fronts, which tend to make fish more active. The key here is stable weather. The more stable the weather for longer periods of time, the more predictable the fish and the fishing. Fish tend to establish more regular feeding patterns during stable weather, making it easier for anglers to figure them out. Keep in mind, too, that fair-weather periods are longer in summer, shorter in spring and fall.

Still, the best time to go fishing is whenever you can. If you have a choice, however, fish during stable, warm-weather fronts—avoid cold fronts—and you'll catch more walleyes.

throw him off," Olson said. "After all, tournament fishing does have its mental aspects."

Aaron McQuoid

After 16 years of guiding on Minnesota's Mille Lacs, Aaron McQuoid moved his operation to Devils Lake, North Dakota. In addition to guiding, McQuoid tournament fished for five years on the FLW tour, and said he has first-hand experience in not doing well on his home waters.

"I'd call it the local-lake disadvantage," Mcquoid said. "What sometimes happened to me, and it happens to others, is that I knew too many good places on my home lake to fish. So I'd end up running from location to location and not spending enough time in just a few spots, fishing those areas thoroughly. And as we all know, you can't catch fish while constantly running 50 miles per hour back and forth across the lake."

McQuoid believes that if you're new to a body of water and you find fish, you'll likely be more consistent in catching them than the locals because you only have a few spots to choose from. Not bad advice from a guy who's learned the hard way that starting your big outboard too often is not always the best decision.

John Gillman

Michigan tournament angler John Gillman takes the opposite view of most other fisherman, believing that fishing home waters can be a benefit—a definite home-field advantage. "In almost every tournament I have fished on Saginaw Bay, I've excelled," Gillman said. "Fishing 'memories' and having many spots to choose from can be a bonus. For instance, if you look at river tournaments on the FLW tour, guys like Nick Johnson and Scott Allar dominate because they know the exact spot-on-the-spot locations to fish."

In Gillman's opinion, it is better to fish locally than to travel and try to figure out new water. "I am way more comfortable at home than anywhere else I fish," he concluded.

Joe Cinelli

A veteran guide of nearly two decades on New York's Niagara River, Lake Ontario, and eastern Lake Erie, Joe Cinelli takes his clients to trophy walleye, as well as salmon and steelhead. He believes that walleyes are some of the most adaptable fish swimming, and walleye anglers need to be just as adaptable to catch them. He recounts the following anecdote as evidence.

"I remember fishing out of Dunkirk, New York, in eastern Lake Erie and finding walleyes in 75 feet of water," Cinelli said. "We pounded them that day, so the next day we went back to that same spot, but couldn't get a bite. Instead of eventually trying a different location, I made the decision to stay in that deep water all day and try to get the fish to go, but with little luck. That evening I talked to some bass fisherman who had limited out on walleyes in just 30 feet of water. What I learned from that episode is that the walleyes had chased the baitfish closer to shore and kept feeding, but I had not adapted."

Mark Martin: Targeting the Largest Walleyes in a Population

Tournament fishing is different from fishing for fun in that tournament anglers are attempting to catch the largest walleyes in a given lake or river system, not just numbers of fish. But learning this targeted approach can be advantageous for all walleye fisherman. Professional angler Mark Martin of Twin Lake, Michigan, explains how he goes about finding, then catching, the largest walleyes in a population.

"First of all, you have to figure out what most of the walleyes in a body of water are doing at any particular time of year," Martin said. "They relate to structure differently and are found in different parts of the lake during different seasons. For instance, in the springtime, are the fish pre-spawn, spawning, or post-spawn? Once you figure out where the majority of walleyes are and what they are doing, you can begin picking away at the larger fish."

Martin went on to say that larger walleyes are usually found deeper in the water column than the smaller fish. "For instance, when fishing a lake reef, I look for larger walleyes to be holding at the base of the reef, especially on days of calmer winds. But as the wind and waves pick up, expect those larger fish to rise in the water column, feeding halfway up or sometimes even just below the surface."

Mark Martin said he catches his largest walleyes by trolling crankbaits. "I believe you will probably catch more walleyes, meaning numbers of fish, slowly trolling night crawler harnesses. But to catch really big walleyes, trolling crankbaits is—hour for hour—the most productive big-fish extracting fishing method I know. And I like fishing large crankbaits, such as Reef Runners and Rapala Deep Husky Jerks, because they seem to target the bigger walleyes."

Change Is the Only Constant . . .

One final point to keep in mind when deciding when and where to fish is that fisheries are always changing. Even though that lake or river you've fished for years may look the same on the surface when you pull up to the boat ramp, beneath the waves is a dynamic system that's constantly in flux. As a result, the techniques and locations that produced fish a year ago, a month ago, a week ago, or possibly even yesterday, may have no bearing on today. It's up to you to decipher the current code. But then, that's what keeps us coming back, now isn't it?

Chapter 7

Early-Spring Trolling

Your Best Chance at a Trophy Walleye

If you need a little convincing as to how productive early-spring walleye trolling can be, listen to this fish story from professional walleye angler Mark Brumbaugh.

"I was pre-fishing for an April tournament on Lake Erie several years ago when a big fish hit," said Brumbaugh. "I knew it was a good one, because the inline planer board went completely underwater. The fish fought hard and felt really heavy as I reeled. I was obviously hoping it was a walleye, but I never expected to net 12 pounds worth—a seven-pounder on the front treble hook of the crankbait and a five-pounder on the rear hook!"

Rich Mealey

Rich Mealey is another Ohio walleye pro with extensive early-season trolling experience on Lake Erie. He specializes in big fish, and his personal best day was five walleyes that totaled a whopping 64.5 pounds!

"Just after the ice leaves is the best time to catch really big walleyes at Erie," said Mealey. "When trolling, I fish just off the Western Basin reefs in about 30 feet of water. The big females leave the reefs after spawning and lie on the bottom for several days, then go on a feeding binge. You may or may not see them on your sonar because they may be too high or too low in the water column, but they're there. They really put on the feed bag with water temperatures between 45 and 50 degrees," he said.

To search for big, early-spring walleyes, Mealey runs his crankbaits back at least 100 feet off inline planer boards—"That 100-foot lead gets big fish," he said—and advises staying away from other boats. "Always run at least one crankbait high in the water column, no more than six feet down," he suggested. "Sometimes big walleyes are so

How productive is early-spring walleye trolling? These two giants were caught from Lake Erie in early April. Holding the fish is Casey Watterson, a professional taxidermist from Mt. Gilead, Ohio.

high in the spring you can actually see them with the naked eye while trolling."

For his trolling equipment, Mealey prefers Model 941 Loomis rods (7½ feet) and Daiwa line-counter reels filled with 15-pound P-Line green monofilament. "Because that line doesn't break," he said. On his outside lines, he fishes crankbaits six to 14 feet down, preferring three main baits: Smithwick Rattlin' Rogues, Reef Runners (both Ripsticks and Deep Divers), and Rapala Deep Husky Jerks. For colors, Mealey likes blue/silver, gold, Firetiger, and black/silver. He attaches his crankbaits to the line with a cross-lock snap (no swivel), and trolls at only about one mile per hour.

On his inside lines, Mealey trolls night crawler harnesses tied with 14-pound test monofilament. "Walleyes will always eat a worm," he reasons. He prefers three #8 treble hooks on his eight-foot harnesses or two single hooks followed by a treble. He then adds a one-quarter to one-ounce keel weight in front of the harness, lets out 30 feet of line, and clips on an inline planer board. He uses a quick-change clevis on his harnesses so that he can easily change size and color of spinner blades.

Mealey also has a tip about inline planer boards. He suggests attaching only the front board clip to the line, rendering the board less stable in the water—more wobbly—making it easier to detect when a fish hits. He also prefers inline planer boards over big boards (skis), as he believes the smaller boards place lures in the water column more precisely.

"It's also easier to change fishing locations with smaller boards rather than larger ones," he said. "And I always troll with the wind. It's easier to 'read' boards while going downwind, and baits run more naturally. Remember, trolling is really nothing more than a controlled drift."

Captain Larry Lambert

Someone who has fished professionally on Lake Erie's famed Western Basin for years is charter captain and tournament angler Larry Lambert, running his boat—Blue 777s—out of Marblehead, Ohio. "I fish for early-season, post-spawn walleyes by trolling around the reefs in the Western Basin," Lambert said. "The theory behind finding big fish early in the year is that the females will come off the spawning reefs and head for deep water, say 28 to 30 feet, and look for a mud bottom. They lay right on the mud for about three days recovering from the spawn, so your sonar may or may not pick them up."

Lambert continued, "These fish don't feed much if at all during that period, but afterwards they begin to suspend off the bottom and go on a feeding frenzy that may last from two to three weeks. And with the large walleye population in Lake Erie, not all the walleyes in the lake

Snow White

If charter boat captain Larry Lambert plans to keep a walleye to eat, he cuts the fish's throat with a small filet knife before placing it in his boat's livewell. As the fish swims in the livewell, it gradually bleeds to death. "The meat will be snow white when you filet that fish," said Lambert. "And if a walleye can taste any better than it already does, it will."

Captain Larry Lambert trolls for Lake Erie walleyes in spring in the deeper water surrounding the many reefs of the Western Basin. This 10-pound trophy was caught on a Reef Runner crankbait.

spawn at the same time. That means the post-spawn bite could last a month or more. Other than during fall, it's an angler's best chance of catching a really big walleye of 10 pounds or heavier," Lambert said.

Larry Lambert specializes in teaching his charter clients how to troll, beginning each trip by giving them a rundown of the tackle he uses. He admits that other brands of equipment work well, too, but the following is what has proven successful and reliable for him through the years: 7½-foot Diawa Heartland rods (medium-light action), Diawa Sealine line-counter reels (model SG27LCA), Off Shore inline planer boards (with OR16 or OR18 clips), Bert's Custom Tackle rod holders, and moss-colored PowerPro braided line (30-pound test, 8-pound diameter).

"After reviewing equipment, the next thing we talk about is always water temperature," Lambert said, "which dictates trolling speed. If the water is between 40 and 55 degrees, I usually troll from 0.5 to 1.0 miles per hour—the warmer the water the faster—and always in a zigzag pattern."

Lambert's three favorite crankbaits for early spring are Smithwick Rattlin' Rogues deep-diver series (ASSRB), Reef Runners (both Deep Divers and Ripsticks), and Rapala Deep Husky Jerks (sizes #10 and

In early spring, stickbaits such as this Rapala Deep Husky Jerk should be trolled slowly, only about one mile per hour. Making slow, wide S-turns with your boat will also help coax a strike from reluctant walleyes.

#12). His go-to colors for Rogues are: blue/chrome/orange belly, clown, and black/gold/orange belly. For Reef Runners: blue Hawaiian, gold clown, Monkey Puke, and Eriedescent. His favorite Rapala colors are: clown, blue/chrome/orange belly, Tennessee shad, and gold/black/orange belly.

As for when to change crankbait colors in the spring, Lambert has developed his own theory. "I believe that catching one walleye on a particular color is suicide on the fish's part or just plain dumb luck on my part," he said. "But if I catch two fish on the same color, to me that equals a pattern. I then switch most or all of my other crankbaits over to that color."

Lambert usually begins his trolling day by running crankbaits back 50 feet off inline planer boards. And if there's an area where stained water meets clearer water—a fishing condition often present in the spring—he'll pilot his boat back and forth between the two areas to see which clarity the fish prefer. At times, he's found baitfish hiding just on the edge of the off-color water and walleyes there, too, feeding on them.

"And keep in mind that walleyes, especially big fish just coming off the spawn, want a meal, not a snack," Lambert said. "That's why I generally use larger-sized baits in the spring." When trolling crankbaits, Lambert prefers them with rattles, believing the noise produced imitates the sound of minnows moving through the water, attracting hungry walleyes.

In addition to crankbaits, Lambert likes to troll an occasional night crawler harness in early spring. "They're a good presentation after the water warms up a little, and they stay productive most of the year," he said. "I run harnesses in one of two ways, either behind a bottom bouncer or behind a Pa's Lure."

Lambert pulls his night crawler harnesses, attached to bottom bouncers, at no more than one mile per hour. "But Pa's Lures can be trolled up to 2.5 miles per hour and still stay down," he said. "The deepest they'll reach is about 22 feet. I modify my Pa's Lures by removing the rear hook and attaching a three-foot night crawler harness." If you're unfamiliar with a Pa's Lure, it looks something like an Erie Dearie—a weight-forward walleye casting lure—only with a diving lip.

Captain Larry Lambert had one last tip. "After spawning in the spring, walleyes have one thing on their minds the rest of the year: feeding. Water temperature dictates where the baitfish will be. During early season the warmer the water, the more baitfish present—and where there are baitfish there are walleyes. If given a choice, I like to fish off-color or dingy water rather than clear water, because baitfish prefer it for better camouflage. And if there is a definite mud line, I'll

Charter captain Larry Lambert clips an Off Shore inline planer board to his trolling line. When purchasing planer boards, keep in mind there are both port (left) and starboard (right) boards; buy an equal number for each side of the boat.

The author, Chip Gross, holds a large, spring-caught walleye. Because the water was murky that day, he chose a chartreuse and silver crankbait with a touch of red, a Rapala Deep Tail Dancer. Photo by Gary Isbell.

try and keep my boat right on the edge of it, trolling half my baits in muddy water and half in clear."

Mark Brumbaugh

Pro walleye angler Mark Brumbaugh fishes crankbaits on Lake Erie in ways similar to Lambert during the spring, but when asked how the technique can be transferred to other bodies of water, he hesitated. "There is no other place exactly like Lake Erie," he said. "A lot of the things I do on Erie won't work on other bodies of water, with the exception of a few large bays on some of the other Great Lakes. It's mainly because of the forage. The big females on Lake Erie suspend and feed both before and after they spawn, but on most other lakes they're hardly ever suspended."

To illustrate, Brumbaugh mentioned a question he often gets while conducting fishing clinics and seminars. Anglers say that they can catch walleyes at Lake Erie, but struggle to catch them from inland lakes.

"That's because on most inland lakes walleyes are not out roaming the middle of the lake as they are at Lake Erie," Brumbaugh said. "They're relating to structure nearer the shoreline, because that's where the forage is, mainly shad. At Erie, walleyes are chasing mostly shiner minnows and other forage found in open water."

Like Larry Lambert, Mark Brumbaugh begins his spring fishing at Lake Erie close to the reef complex in the Western Basin as soon as the ice leaves. He follows the contour lines around the perimeter of individual reefs, and said that when he first began using a Navionics chip in his Lowrance electronics he was amazed at how often his previous waypoints lined up on specific contour lines.

Brumbaugh always keeps at least one crankbait high when spring trolling, in the top 10 feet of the water column. He knows that during

Does Spring Surface Temperature Really Matter?

It was a sunny, April morning several years ago when I first fished with Captain Larry Lambert on Lake Erie, but the water temperature was still only in the mid-30s following a very cold winter and later-than-normal spring. We started trolling about mid-morning, yet after several hours had caught nothing, not even a non-target fish.

It wasn't until mid-afternoon, when surface water temperatures bumped up to around 40 degrees, that we hit a cooperative school of walleyes. During the next two hours we caught two walleyes at 2½ pounds, a 5-pounder, and a 10-pound-plus trophy. We also lost two other nice walleyes that came unbuttoned near the boat.

The point is not to give up too early in the day during the spring, especially if the sun is shining. Sometimes, just a few degrees' jump in surface water temperature can make all the difference. But I've seen just the opposite happen, as well. I was fishing Lake Erie early one April when a buddy and I boated a 29-inch and 30-inch walleye (both spawned-out females) within 20 minutes of each other about mid-morning, our first hour on the water. Yet we trolled back and forth over that same area the remainder of the day and never caught another fish of any kind. Go figure. . . .

the spring the warmest water is near the surface, drawing the most active fish to that level. "I mark a lot of fish deep during spring, but most of the walleyes I actually catch are up high," he said. "If I want to go after deep fish, I usually jig for them, not troll."

One last tip Brumbaugh offers when spring crankbait trolling for walleyes is to occasionally let your lures come to a complete stop in the water. "Sometimes walleyes want the crankbait absolutely still," he said. "That's when I like the Off Shore Tattle Flags on my inline planer boards, because they act just like a bobber. When I stop a board and a flag goes down, I turn the boat in the opposite direction, give it some gas, tighten up the line, and reel in the fish."

If you need one last bit of convincing as to how productive early-season trolling can be, the walleye on the cover of this book was caught at Lake Erie in late March and weighed a whopping 11.7 pounds, my personal best walleye ever! My fishing buddy and I had to literally dodge ice floes that day with our trolling lines, but it was well worth the effort. In just three hours, we caught a total of eight walleyes that collectively weighed a few ounces shy of 50 pounds.

Chapter 8

A Shot in the Dark

Night-Trolling for Walleyes

I never knew how productive night-trolling for walleyes could be until two Lake Erie veterans took me under their collective wing and showed me the ropes firsthand. It was a night of spring fishing I'll never forget.

"It's my opinion that the excellent night fishing happens in spring all along the southern shore of the lake, not just in our area," said Den Braun. At the time, Braun was the owner of a bait and tackle shop in Vermilion, Ohio. He's since retired from that business, as well as retiring his charter captain's license. He now fishes mainly for fun, with charter captain Bob Hanmer, who runs his 28-foot Proline (*Rebel Queen*) from a marina on the Vermilion River.

"The night-trolling bite starts when the water temperature reaches about 46 degrees," said Braun. "That's usually about mid- to late April, and the good fishing lasts three to four weeks. By the time the water warms to 62 degrees, it's usually over."

Braun believes that Lake Erie walleyes spawn not only in tributary rivers and on lake reefs, but also along the shoreline. "We catch mainly male walleyes at night during the spring of the year," Braun said, "and most of the fish will be flowing with milt when we land them. But even though they are not as big as the females we catch later in the year in this area, our average fish is still 22 to 23 inches, or about three to four pounds."

So why can't anglers catch those same walleyes during daylight hours in the spring? "That's the $64,000 question—I just don't know," said Captain Bob Hanmer. "We can catch smallmouth bass all day long during the spring in the same area and maybe a few walleyes, but no great numbers of 'eyes to speak of. But when the sun goes down, those smallies quit feeding and the walleyes turn on. I don't know if they've been out in deep water during the day and move in to feed or they have been lying on the bottom in the shallows, but all of a sudden they start feeding. It's amazing how it happens."

Den Braun of Vermilion, Ohio, lands a night-caught walleye. Notice Braun's headlamp, which leaves his hands free for reeling, netting, and handling fish.

How shallow is the springtime night bite? Hanmer starts trolling at a water depth of only seven to eight feet. "Which is only a quarter-mile to half-mile off shore," said Hanmer. "I run my baits five to six feet down in the water column. And if I don't pick up any fish, I'll even try running my boat shallower before going deeper. Unfortunately, I've paid the price for that a time or two by bumping a shallow rock pile with my prop."

Hanmer's night-trolling program includes running two lines per person, spread to the side of the boat by Off Shore inline planer boards. The boards are individually lighted so that each one is easily visible in the dark.

Hanmer's trolling rods are seven-foot, two-piece Shimanos (model TDR 1703) mated with Okuma line-counter reels (model 20 DX). Hanmer likes 30-pound test PowerPro braided line, not only for its strength, but also for its thin diameter. He attaches his baits—he trolls nothing but large crankbaits in spring—directly to the line with cross-lock snap swivels, forgoing any type of leader.

Top-producing crankbaits for this kind of springtime night walleye trolling include Rapala Husky Jerks, Smithwick Rattlin' Rogues, and Reef Runner Ripsticks. The Husky Jerks Hanmer likes to run from 26

Small-lipped stickbaits are good choices for trolling shallow walleyes, especially at night.

to 30 feet back from his inline planer boards, Rogue's 35 feet back, and Ripsticks 18 to 22 feet back. His favorite colors of Husky Jerk include blue/chrome, glass perch, glass minnow, and clown; in Rogues he prefers blue/chrome and clown; for Ripsticks try rainbow, mooneye, Eriedescent, black/chrome, blue/chrome, and any of the prism colors.

Hanmer and First Mate Braun begin trolling at dusk at about 1.7 to 1.8 miles per hour, adjusting the boat's speed up or down slightly as the fish dictate on any particular night. To slow Hanmer's big Proline to those slower speeds, he drags Amish-made "Buggy Bag" trolling socks, one tied off to each side of the boat.

"The fishing can be good all night long," said Hanmer, "but usually the first few hours after dark are consistently the best. And wave action doesn't seem to matter like it often does during daylight walleye fishing. It can be flat calm out there at night and we'll still catch fish. In fact, flat-calm nights have made for some of our best fishing."

How good can night fishing be? On the evening I first fished aboard the *Rebel Queen* in early May several years ago, three of us caught our 18-walleye limit in just two hours. There was seldom a time when there wasn't a fish being fought and landed, and at times we had doubles to contend with, and one triple-header. The walleyes easily averaged four pounds apiece that night, so we went home with over 70 pounds of fish. And what was even more amazing is that we did not catch a single other species—it was pure walleyes, start to finish.

Such was my introduction to night walleye trolling, and I've since learned that the technique can be used during any open-water season of the year: spring, summer, or fall. In fact, in some lakes trolling at night is about the only way to consistently catch walleyes during the hot summer months when warm water temperatures and direct sunlight push walleyes into hiding during the day. So how do you get started fishing after dark? In addition to the regular trolling equipment already discussed in Chapters Two and Three, here's what you'll need.

Basic Night-time Equipment: Lights and Lots of Them

This may seem like a no-brainer, but when I first began walleye trolling at night I noticed that after sunset it got real dark—real dark, real quick. And if I wasn't properly prepared, I couldn't see much. (Duh!) Like I said, it should have been obvious to me, but it wasn't. And my night vision has never been good, which only complicated the problem.

Murphy's Night Law: After Dark, Whatever Can Go Wrong Will Go Wrong!

If you've never fished at night on big water, especially during the cold-water periods of the year—spring and fall—both Den Braun and Captain Bob Hanmer emphasize the need for caution and preparation. "You should thoroughly check out the area you're going to fish *before* dark to become familiar with it," said Braun. "And don't have anything lying loose in your boat that you won't immediately need. Stow it away. Because if anything can go wrong after dark, it likely will."

Another tip from this pair of veteran fishermen is to tape a flashlight to the handle of your landing net. The light comes in handy not only when netting fish, but also while working the hooks out of fish and the net once walleyes are landed.

That said, I've since learned what it takes to be efficient while walleye trolling at night, the main ingredient being various types of dependable, artificial lights. Notice I said *dependable.* You don't want to gamble your long-awaited fishing trip—or possibly your safety—on less-than-adequate equipment, so buy quality lights and a backup or two.

I no longer venture onto the water after dark without an assortment of sizes of flashlights (I like the heavy-duty Maglite brand used by law enforcement officers), as well as assorted headlamps, and, of course, the proper boat lights, both navigational and interior. And speaking of boat lights, some anglers include a high-intensity spotlight for added illumination when hunting the boat ramp in the dark to put the boat back on the trailer.

Headlamps are handy because they strap to your head with an elastic band, leaving your hands free. The lamp itself is positioned on your forehead, so wherever you look the light beam is focused on that spot. Most headlamps are relatively inexpensive, $20 or less, so buy several, as you never know when one may conk out or you might lose one overboard. It also helps to have an extra or two on hand for buddies you invite along. If they are unfamiliar with night fishing, they may or may not think to bring a headlamp of their own. And it should go without saying that you need to carry extra, fresh batteries for all your lights.

You'll also need lights on your inline planer boards. Some boards, such as the Off Shore brand, have lights that can be swapped out with the board's flag. It's a simple matter of screwing off the flag and screwing on the light. The lights can even be purchased in red for running on the port (left) side of the boat, and green for running on the starboard (right) side. This color coding is a courtesy to other boats that might be trolling in the same area, as it's easier for them to tell which direction you're headed.

Here's a money-saving tip: if you don't already have lights for your inline planer boards and want to give night-trolling a try, chemical glow sticks can be substituted in a pinch. Just duct tape or wire one glow stick to the flag of each of your boards, and you're in business. Chemical glow sticks produce light for hours and are inexpensive.

There is something very unique and relaxing about night-trolling for walleyes, especially on a moonlit night. Relaxing, that is, until one of your planer board lights starts dancing on the water, signaling the

Peter Gross hoists a night-caught walleye using a fish gripper, keeping his hand away from the fish's toothy mouth.

Lighted planer boards are a necessity for night walleye trolling. Make sure to have extra batteries aboard for all of your lights.

first fish of the evening. Give night-trolling a try and you'll soon learn what I mean. Just make sure you go properly prepared.

Hope you're a night owl. . . .

Chapter 9

Taking the Plunge

Purchasing and Rigging a Boat for Walleye Trolling

All the walleye fishing information and insider knowledge contained in the chapters of this book will be worthless without a stable, safe platform from which to troll: your boat. Dave Rose of Grawn, Michigan, is a professional, multispecies fishing guide specializing in chasing walleyes. He's also an outdoors writer and author of the book *The Fishing Boat,* published by The Lyons Press. The book is subtitled, *Use the Secrets of the Pros to Select and Outfit Your Boat.* Not surprisingly, Rose has a boatload—just couldn't resist the pun—of valuable information to share about purchasing and rigging a walleye boat for trolling.

Aluminum or Fiberglass?

The first decision a walleye angler has to make when purchasing a boat for trolling concerns the hull material: aluminum or fiberglass. "I personally like aluminum," said Rose, "because I can beach the boat if I need to and not have to worry about damaging the hull. Fiberglass, on the other hand, gives a smoother ride on big water, cutting through the waves better than aluminum because it's a heavier material, adding weight to the boat."

Rose said that a heavier boat is also not affected as much by wind. "The wind doesn't catch it and blow it around as readily. If you're going to be fishing primarily big water, mainly on the Great Lakes or large reservoirs, I'd suggest purchasing fiberglass," Rose said.

Storage Space

Another important consideration when purchasing a boat is whether or not it has adequate storage space. "You can never have enough storage compartments," said Rose. "You don't want equipment such as extra

Walleye trolling boats for big water should be at least 17 feet in length and have a deep-vee hull design. Note the three motors on this boat: main motor, gas-powered "kicker" trolling motor, and bow-mounted electric trolling motor.

tackle, ice chests, anchor and line, life jackets, and other items cluttering the deck. And remember, there is no such thing as totally dry storage on a boat, only areas of relative dampness. So when you return home after a fishing trip always open all the hatches, storage compartments, rod lockers, live wells, etc., to let air circulate and dry them out."

Rose strongly suggests actually getting in a boat you're considering buying and test driving it. How fast does it go, and also how slow? Is it responsive when you hit the throttle, or does it wallow coming out of the hole? Is it stable or a bit tippy when you walk around? Is there adequate room for trolling equipment and are the gunnels wide enough for mounting rod holders? Is the transom area easily accessible for netting fish? In short, does the boat you're considering buying have everything you're looking for?

"There is no perfect boat," admits Rose, "but if you can find a boat that has about 80 percent of the features you're after, it *might* be the boat for you. But it might not be, too, so take your time in making a boat-buying decision."

Personally, I looked at walleye boats for a couple of years before buying my Yar-Craft, new, and I've not regretted the purchase. It's a bare-bones walleye trolling rig, but the boat-motor-trailer combination does everything I ask of it, and does it in a rugged, dependable, good-looking package.

New vs. Used

If you don't have the budget for a new boat, an advantage of buying used is that you can try the boat for a year or two, fish from it, and if you find it doesn't meet your needs you can always resell it for about the same amount of money you bought it. Purchasing a new boat, on the other hand, does not offer that same option. Buy new, and it's like driving a new car or truck off the dealer's showroom floor—the boat loses several thousand dollars in value the minute you take possession. So if you're just getting started in walleye trolling, you may want to buy a used boat first; then once you've learned the ropes and are more in tune with what all is involved, purchase a new boat. The decision's ultimately up to you.

What about the Trailer?

"Buy a quality, heavy-duty trailer to transport your boat, and you won't regret it," said Dave Rose. "And keep in mind when selecting a trailer that the boat should come off the trailer easily and go on easily. And that's another reason for test-driving a boat. You have the opportunity to see how the trailer performs at the boat ramp."

Many trailers today are custom-manufactured for specific boats, which is a great advantage. The boat sits on the trailer well, your vehicle will be able to tow the boat easier—saving gas—and ultimately you'll be happier with your trailer's overall performance.

What about bunks versus rollers on a trailer? Rollers may load and unload a boat easier than bunks, but bunks support a boat's hull better. That is especially important with fiberglass boats, because of their weight. Rollers also tend to continually wear and dent an aluminum hull in the same areas, especially if you trailer your boat often and for long distances.

Minimum Size

How small is too small for walleye trolling on the Great Lakes? "A 17-foot boat is about minimum length," said Rose. "Trolling can be done from a 16- or even a 14-footer close to shore, but if you seriously want to fish big water, your boat should be at least a 17-footer with a deep-vee hull design." A 17-foot boat provides room for three anglers, comfortably, with one person driving and two manning the trolling lines and netting fish. Rose went on to say that an advantage of a 17-footer over a larger craft is that one person can launch and retrieve a boat of that size alone, if necessary.

Keep in mind, however, that a small boat on the Great Lakes is still just that, a small boat. "I've had my boat 12 miles out in Lake Superior," Rose said, "and you feel pretty small out there." For the record, Rose guides from a 17.5-foot, aluminum-hulled MirroCraft, with Johnson outboard engines for both his main motor and gas-powered "kicker."

Motors

Main motors: "As to a boat's main motor—its primary power source—you always want to max-out the horsepower of the motor for the rating of the boat, or get as close to the maximum rating as you possibly can," advises Rose. "For instance, my boat is rated for a main motor of 150 horsepower. The most horsepower I could buy at the time in a Johnson outboard without going over the 150 rating limit of the boat was a 140 horsepower, so that's what I bought."

Rose went on to explain that the reason you want the largest possible motor for your boat is that top-end speed of a boat-motor combination is extremely important. "It's important in getting you where you plan to fish sooner rather than later," he said, "translating into

This solo walleye angler is using his tiller-operated main motor to troll upstream, against a strong current, in Michigan's Grand River.

more fishing time. But speed is also important in allowing you to get off the water just as quickly, should a storm start brewing."

He also points out that having a main engine maxed in horsepower for the particular boat you'll be fishing is a gas saver, as the motor will not labor as hard to push the boat through the water. "Get your boat up on plane as quickly as you can, then back off the throttle a little, and you'll save on fuel consumption, possibly as much as 30 percent," said Rose. "Outboard motors are expensive, there is no getting around that, but matching a motor to your boat is critical, so don't skimp on horsepower."

Gas-powered trolling motors: If you choose to add a gas-powered "kicker" outboard trolling motor to your boat's transom, you'll want it to move the boat slowly enough for serious walleye trolling. "And that's where some people make a mistake and buy too large a trolling motor, meaning too high a horsepower," said Rose. "For instance, on my 17-foot MirroCraft I have a 9.9-horsepower gas-powered trolling motor, but could have probably gotten by with a six-horse."

Ideally, for walleye fishing, you want a kicker that has the ability to troll at a minimum speed of one mile per hour or less. A kicker motor is also cheap insurance that, should your main motor not start or malfunction for some reason while on the water, the second motor will get you back to shore. It may do so slowly, but you'll make it back to the dock.

Dave Rose recalls having his starting battery quit one day while fishing, rendering his main motor useless. "My big motor wouldn't even turn over, let alone start," said Rose. "What I did to remedy the situation was pull-start my 9.9 kicker, count to 60, then try to start my main motor. Because there is a 40-amp alternator in the kicker, it generated enough electricity to allow the big motor to start. That little trick saved the day, so keep it in mind if you have both of your motors—the main motor and kicker—wired to the same staring battery."

Electric trolling motors: As with a boat's main motor, Rose advises buying the most power you can afford when purchasing an electric trolling motor, and in addition getting the longest shaft available. "You'll need that extra shaft length when the wind picks up," said Rose. "A short-shaft may work well during times of relatively flat seas, but when waves kick up and the boat's bow starts bouncing up and down,

A small, gas-powered "kicker" motor (left) is used to slow a boat to trolling speed. It's also insurance that, should your main motor quit working for some reason, you will be able to return to the dock.

a bow-mounted electric trolling motor needs a long shaft to keep its propeller in the water."

Not all electric trolling motors are bow-mounted, however. Some are made to mount on a boat's transom or even on the lower unit of the main motor. But electric motors mounted at the rear of a boat don't provide as much steering control as those mounted on the bow, as it is always easier for a motor to pull a boat rather than push it. A good analogy here is a car with front-wheel versus rear-wheel drive.

A very handy feature now available on Minn-Kota electric trolling motors is a technology known as iPilot, allowing hands-free and feet-free operation of a trolling motor from anywhere in the boat—electronically and wirelessly—using a simple key fob. If you're in the market for an electric trolling motor, check it out.

Rod Holders

"The number one most important concern in rigging a walleye boat for efficient and effective trolling is placement of the rod holders," said Rose. "And to do so, there is no substitute for getting in your boat and moving around like you would when you are actually fishing. If

Tips to Keep in Mind when Boat Shopping:

- **Wood, Aluminum, or Fiberglass?**—There are advantages and disadvantages to all three of these boat hull materials, but, in general, the first-time boat owner would probably do best to choose either aluminum or fiberglass, as wooden boats take a significant amount of upkeep and yearly maintenance.
- **Don't Be in a Hurry**—Do your homework and give yourself plenty of time when deciding on a boat purchase. You will likely own the boat for years, so don't make a hasty decision you may later regret. If a salesperson pressures you to "buy today," walk away.
- **Ask Lots of Questions**—Don't know the difference between a two-stroke and four-stroke outboard motor? Can't tell a tiller from a trailer? Ask. Boating has its own jargon, and nautical terms can be confusing for the newcomer. The only dumb question is not the one you don't know the answer to, it's the one you don't ask.
- **Is All Safety Equipment Included in the Purchase Price?**—Life jackets, anchor and line, fire extinguisher, flares, distress flag, all of this required safety equipment will cost you several hundred additional dollars if it's not included in the selling price of the boat. It may not be, but it doesn't hurt to inquire.
- **Don't Forget Boat Insurance**—One of the most overlooked costs when considering buying a boat is insurance. It's usually inexpensive, but it does pay to shop around to find the best coverage available at the best price. Don't leave the dock, or your driveway, without it.

you do this in your driveway with the neighbors watching, they will likely think you're weird, but do it anyway. It's that important."

A few questions to ask yourself during this make-believe fishing trip should include the following. Will you be sitting or standing in your boat most of the time while trolling? Will the rods be easily accessible if the rod holders are placed where you're contemplating installing them? Will a rod butt be in the way if a hatch door is opened? Will a transom-mounted trolling motor arm interfere with a rod holder or rod butt if the motor is tilted up? And any number of other questions.

Think through as many of the above-mentioned scenarios as possible. Once you've answered those questions, install as many rod-holder bases on your boat as you can afford, assuring that you can move rod holders around to various locations. For instance, if you have six rod holders, you may want to install 10 to 12 rod-holder bases, giving you more options and more versatility in your fishing.

Some rod holders attach to a track system, whereby individual rod holders slide along the track and can be positioned anywhere along that line you want them. As for reliable name brands, Dave Rose uses Cannon rod holders on his boat, while I use those manufactured by Bert's Custom Tackle. It doesn't matter what brand name you choose as long as the rod holders are heavy duty, solidly anchored, and can take some punishment.

For instance, while walleye trolling, your rods and lines may be pulling diving devices, inline planer boards, inline weights, or other heavy tackle in addition to a lure; all that equipment can put a lot of strain on a rod holder. In addition, a 15-pound steelhead or 20-pound salmon may hit your lure instead of a walleye. Could your rod holders take that kind of stress and strain? Make sure they can.

And take your time deciding not only where to place rod holders, but on the installation process as well. Don't rush or cut corners here. The old adage, "Measure twice, cut once," is paramount, because once you drill a hole in your boat, you can't undo it; that hole is there to stay.

"But once I decide where I want to mount rod holders or other equipment, I love drilling holes in my boat," said Rose. "Because that means I'm getting closer to actually going fishing. So once you've made up your mind and measured accurately, go for it. Don't be shy."

Electronics

When it comes to rigging a walleye trolling boat with electronics, you want to purchase the most powerful unit(s) you can afford; however, it is possible to go overboard. For instance, low-priced, mid-priced, and high-priced GPS/sonar units all essentially do the same things. Your decision, then, boils down to how many extra features you want—or how many you can afford—and the size of the display screen.

Dave Rose has a Humminbird 700 Series GPS/sonar unit mounted to the bow of his boat, and a 900 series on the dash. He admits these units may not be top of the line, but are still very powerful with clear screens that are easy to read. "Actually, I think the 700 series Humminbird is *the* best unit I've ever owned," said Rose, "powerful, easy to use, and easy to see the screen."

In general, Rose advises, “If you have a larger boat, you should also have a larger screen for your GPS/sonar unit so that you can see it easily from anywhere in the boat.” Rose’s screens are large enough that he can divide the displays in half, showing the GPS map function on one side and sonar on the other.

“Boat control is critical in walleye trolling,” said Rose, “and good electronics allow you to do just that, accurately position your boat. For instance, if you catch walleyes along a certain trolling route, the GPS function allows you to retrace that route exactly.”

Side-Scan Sonar

A relatively new feature recently available on sonar units is side-scan capability. In other words, some sonar units now scan to the side of the boat as well as directly beneath it. But is side-scan sonar absolutely necessary? In a word, no. Anglers have been catching walleyes for years without it. However, the technology will help you find bottom structure that you didn’t know was there unless you happened to drive your boat directly over it. “Side-scan sonar allows you to see a crevice or boulder

Quality electronics are essential to modern-day walleye trolling. Some anglers prefer separate screens for their GPS and sonar units, while others prefer splitting a single screen, which saves space on the boat. Pictured is a Lowrance combination unit set to split screen mode; the map display is on the left and sonar display on the right.

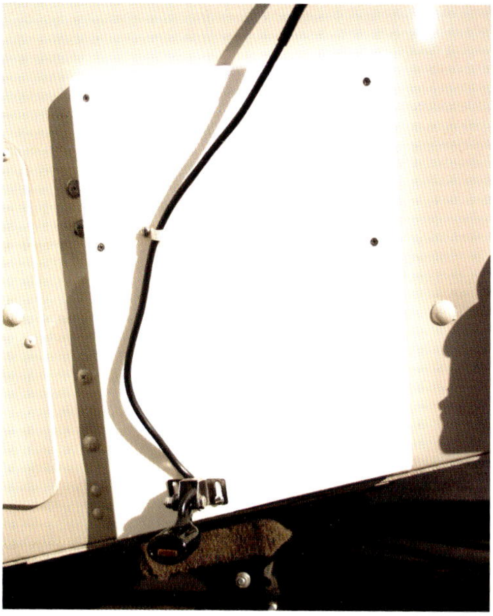

Professional walleye guide Dave Rose mounts the transducer of his sonar unit on a plastic board before screwing the board to the transom of his boat above the waterline. This helps keep the boat watertight.

located on a reef the first time you drive by," said Rose. "It's handy because the technology lets you see things that are not on any map."

Rose's sonar unit can scan up to about 250 feet on each side of his boat, but he usually keeps the sensitivity level set at about the 150-foot mark, which seems to give him the clearest picture. This relatively recent technology is constantly being improved and upgraded, so if you're buying new electronics, make sure to investigate the side-scan capabilities of the unit you're considering.

Along those same lines, a concern when rigging a boat for walleye trolling is how to mount a transducer for sonar units. Dave Rose does not like to drill any holes in his boat below the waterline, believing that's just asking for problems. How, then, does he mount his sonar transducers? He first attaches a transducer to a plastic board—a board about a foot wide, 18 inches long, and half an inch thick—then attaches the board to his boat's transom by placing several screws *above* the boat's waterline. It's a simple solution to a tricky problem, but one that helps keep a boat watertight.

Weather Radar

Another electronic feature Rose employs on his boat is XM Satellite Radar Weather. "In my line of work as a professional fishing guide, it's good to know whether that large, black cloud I can see in the distance is moving toward me or away from me, and that I can get myself and my clients safely back to the dock without getting wet, or worse. Dependable, up-to-the-minute weather information is especially important on the vast, open waters of the Great Lakes where storms can kick up suddenly and build huge waves within minutes." The current cost of this technology is about $10 per month, and may be a wise safety investment, depending upon where you fish.

Dave Rose has one final bit of advice about rigging a walleye boat for trolling. "Walleyes like cold weather and cold water, but everything else on your boat does not," he said. "So having reliable equipment and installing and maintaining it properly will allow you to fish when the fishing gets good, not be stuck at the dock making repairs."

Advice from Captain Peg

Captain Peg Van Vleet of Huber Heights, Ohio, is an angler who has owned three boats during her lifetime. Peg has fished Lake Erie for 40 years, the last decade as a professional charter boat captain. Her current boat is a 28-foot Baha Cruiser named the *Blue Diamond*.

"I would advise anyone buying a walleye fishing boat to first make a list of the features he or she wants and doesn't want," Peg said. "A good way to decide what those things are is to visit the waterway you plan to fish most often and actually see what boats are common there. And if you are going to fish on big water, such as the Great Lakes, size does matter—the bigger the boat the better. But an angler should also keep in mind seamanship skills. You need to feel comfortable in the boat you'll be handling."

Take a Safe Boating Course!

As with driving cars and trucks there are "rules of the road" that apply to boating. Spending a few hours in a classroom learning these rules and how to operate a boat safely could save your life—or at least spare you some serious embarrassment while on the water or at the boat ramp. For a list of boating courses available in your area, contact the U.S. Coast Guard Auxiliary, U.S. Power Squadron, or your state or provincial department of natural resources. Some states now require mandatory training for first-time boat operators, regardless of age.

Captain Peg Van Vleet has been fishing Lake Erie for 40 years, and has some good advice for anglers looking to buy a boat for walleye trolling.

"When considering buying a used boat," Peg continued, "check each detail, both inside and out, as it will give you hints as to how well the boat has been maintained. For example, if the boat has an engine—outboard, inboard/outboard, or inboard—is there excess oil around the motor or possibly even an oil leak? Is there water in the bilge area? Check the hull exterior for any nicks, chips, cracks, or dings. And ask about any previous major repairs. Also, try and find out why the owner is selling. If it's a guy, talk to his wife," Peg grinned. "She'll usually give you the straight scoop as to why the boat's up for sale."

Captain Peg added that if you feel the least bit uncomfortable inspecting a used boat yourself, hiring a professional to do the job for you is a wise alternative. Ask around for a marine surveyor with a good reputation who will give you an honest, unbiased boat evaluation and appraisal. Make sure to discuss the extent of the inspection—known as a pre-purchase survey—and its cost *before* giving a surveyor the go-ahead. And NEVER use a surveyor recommended by the seller. The boat in question should be out of the water for a thorough inspection. Also insist that the inspection results be provided to you in writing as well as verbally.

In addition, Peg suggests trying out the boat on the water as well as on the road. “Sit at the helm and take a look around. Can you see 360 degrees? Are the wheel or tiller and throttle in a convenient place for you? If the boat has gauges or electronics screens, can you view them all easily? If possible, take the boat for a spin. How does it handle at various speeds, cutting through waves, and in reverse? And, if possible, tow the boat, motor, and trailer with your tow vehicle. How does it handle when going up and down hills, changing lanes, and backing? Finally, remember that your search for a boat—new or used—is a very personal decision, so take your time, do your homework, and don’t settle for just any boat.”

Chapter 10

What's a Trophy Walleye?

The fish weighed more than 12 pounds—well over the 10-pound mark most anglers consider a true trophy walleye, even by Great Lakes standards. It was a female, having hatched more than 20 years ago from a tiny egg, deposited and fertilized in Lake Erie's Western Basin, the Walleye Capital of the World.

The exact location was Niagara Reef, about halfway between the famed Bass Islands and the lake's western shoreline. The yellow egg lay beneath basketball-sized rocks along the bottom for several weeks—along with tens of thousands of other walleye eggs—while the spring sun gradually warmed the water day after day until the microscopic fish finally came to life.

But even before hatching, the tiny walleye faced peril. Round gobies and other egg-eating fish regularly patrolled Niagara Reef, sucking down as many walleye eggs and those of other species as they could find. Small, invasive predators, measuring no more than about six inches long, round gobies were accidentally introduced to the Great Lakes in the late twentieth century through the ballast water of ocean-going freighters, known as "salties." Since then, goby numbers had exploded in the lake, and the particular walleye egg containing the female fish was lucky to have escaped their notice. Many of its siblings had not.

One warm afternoon, the walleye finally wriggled free of her rubbery egg case, officially becoming a fry, and lay on the bottom cobble rocks of the reef, recovering from her struggle. She survived on her egg sac the first several days, an extended bulge of nutrients protruding from her belly. When hunger finally forced her to seek food, she began instinctively feeding on microscopic animals known as zooplankton, beginning her lifelong role as a predator.

Because the amount of plankton in the water of Lake Erie is very prolific, the young walleye began to grow quickly. By the end of the

What's a trophy walleye? Ten pounds...? Twelve pounds...? Only you can decide.

summer she was already eight inches long, now feeding on young-of-the-year of other fish species. By age two, she had doubled her length to 16 inches.

After a decade of life, the female walleye was 26 inches long and weighed just shy of six pounds. And during those 10 years she had survived many threats to her life. She had been pursued time and again by larger fish, escaping each encounter. One time, however, during her first summer, she just barely avoided death.

A large smallmouth bass, a male weighing well over five pounds and measuring more than twice the walleye's length, had spotted her cruising toward him along a rocky drop-off. She was swimming with others of her species, but on the outside of the small school of walleyes.

When the school was within striking distance, the bass suddenly rushed from the cover of rocks and slashed into the school, mouth agape. Walleye fingerlings instinctively scattered in all directions like flashes of light in the water. The young female tried to follow, but found herself caught and held by the tail. The smallmouth had the bottom, white tip of her caudal fin in his mouth, the strong grip of his sandpaper-like jaws holding her fast.

Sensing she had one last chance at survival, the female walleye flared her dorsal and pectoral fins and fought with all her strength to free herself, twisting and turning in every direction. But the bass had not grown as large as he was by being an inefficient predator. He suddenly opened his mouth and flared his gills, attempting to suck her the remainder of the way into his maw with a rush of water, as he had done thousands of times before with other prey fish.

Feeling herself being flushed backward into the vortex of the bass's gullet, the walleye arched her body to the left and swam with all her might. Luckily, she bounced off the smallmouth's upper jaw, and before he could recover to make another strike she was gone. Swimming as fast as she could toward the bottom of the lake and deeper, darker water, she quickly joined another school of her own kind and size.

Predatory birds had also tried to eat the female walleye several times when she was young. Gulls didn't dive below the surface, and she had been able to see them coming and quickly move out of range. But double-crested cormorants were a different danger. These large, fish-eating birds were well adapted to chasing fish below the surface, and had eaten thousands of her siblings. Once, a cormorant had even gotten so close that its serrated bill had raked her side, knocking off several scales and drawing a drop or two of blood. She carried a permanent scar on her right flank as a result of that encounter, but the wound had quickly healed. She was none the worse for wear because of it, but wiser about swimming into clear, shallow water, especially when she could see dark forms moving in the sky above.

That had been many years ago. More than 20 years old now, the walleye was an apex predator, and there was very little in the lake she feared. Her time was spent alternately feeding and resting. If there was sufficient oxygen on the bottom of the lake, she preferred loafing there, especially during summer days when the sunlight was more intense, her belly flat to the cool mud. If the bottom was anoxic, she'd suspend about halfway up in the water column, just above the thermocline. There, the water temperature was still relatively cool, yet she had enough oxygen to breathe comfortably.

It was at that level, about midway down, where she was this day. It was late August, and she was in the waters of Lake Erie's Central Basin, having migrated east from the warmer water of the Western Basin in early June. Sometimes she swam in a loose school with other large walleyes and sometimes not. She had become more solitary the older and larger she had grown. Today she was by herself, occasionally feeding on emerald shiner minnows, gulping them down one by one like candy.

She'd fill her air bladder and slowly rise toward the surface, watching for schools of baitfish in the water column as she did so. Upon spotting a ball of minnows—actually sensing their presence in the water with the lateral line down her side before seeing them—she'd slowly herd them toward the surface, then quickly propel herself into the small school with a sweep of her broad, powerful tail. Each time she did, a tasty shiner ended up in her gullet.

Taking a break to rest again, it was late afternoon when she felt the gnawing need to feed once more. During this time of year she fed many hours of the day. Her body being cold-blooded, its metabolism always revved up in the warmer waters of summer, slowing down in winter.

As she slowly rose toward the surface again, she heard a noise; a noise that grew progressively louder. She had heard that same noise all her life on Lake Erie, and it was always followed by the shadow of a large object passing overhead on the surface of the water. She had no way of knowing the shadow was a boat. A boat containing fishermen. She only knew that the noisy objects were more prevalent this time of year, summer, less so during spring and fall; practically nonexistent in winter.

She stopped her ascent to let the noisy object pass, then continued toward the surface. The large, female walleye sensed small objects coming toward her in the water. Could they be baitfish? They sounded like it, but the sound was not quite what she was used to. Curious now, she continued to let herself rise in the water column, her predatory instincts kicking into high gear.

It was a sunny day with large, puffy, white clouds hanging in the late-afternoon summer sky. The sun penetrated deeply into the flat, waveless water, and she first saw the minnow as a flash of gold. It moved slowly, only about two miles per hour, and was by itself, not in a school, which was odd. But the large walleye didn't hesitate. If she didn't eat this lone minnow, she knew another of her kind soon would. She rose to follow.

Closing the distance to the emerald shiner, it didn't look quite like the other minnows she'd been feeding on that day, but it was obviously injured. The small fish fluttered and twisted in the water, its sides flashing gold with each glint of the sun. She quickened her pace and swam just a couple of feet behind the minnow for several minutes, inspecting it, seeing if it was healthy enough to try and make an escape. It didn't. The minnow simply kept its steady, struggling pace until she could resist its temptations no longer. With a quick flip of her tail she shot forward, opened her large, toothy mouth, and inhaled the four-inch-long, hammered-gold metal trolling spoon.

Instantly, the large female walleye knew something was wrong, but by then it was too late. The wickedly sharp number four treble hook at the rear of the lure had already buried itself deeply into the corner of her bony jaw. There was no escape.

"There's one, Dad!" a fisherman on the boat that had just passed above said, pointing to the yellow planer board now dancing on the surface of the water.

"About time . . . ," the older man growled, slowly rising from his seat to pull the trolling rod from its holder. "It's been a good hour since our last fish, and that one was a sheephead."

Below the surface, the large walleye was fighting for her life, diving for deeper water while at the same time trying to dislodge the object stinging her jaw. She opened and closed her mouth repeatedly and shook her head continually as she swam, but to no avail. And to make matters worse, she was beginning to feel herself being dragged forward through the water.

"Wow, this feels like a big one!" the old man said as he began reeling. "Just hope it's a walleye and not another dang sheephead."

"I'll take the board off for you, Dad," the younger man said. "Whenever you *finally* get it to the boat," he teased.

"Hey, I told you this was a big fish," the old man defended. "I'm gonna take my time. Don't wanna lose it. Put the motor in neutral to help me get this fish started toward the boat, will ya?"

The younger man obeyed his father's suggestion, pulling the throttle lever of the boat backward until the outboard motor slipped out of gear, slowly stopping the boat's forward momentum. The female walleye felt the tension on the line ease slightly and took advantage of it, making yet another dive toward the bottom with all her strength.

"Look at that!" yelled the older man, pointing with his chin behind the boat. "That planer board went completely underwater. . . . I told you this was a big fish!"

"Take your time, Dad. You don't want to lose this one."

"Don't tell me how to fight a fish. I've caught more walleyes in my lifetime than you'll ever hope to."

The younger man knew his father was right. He had fished with his dad for years, ever since he was a kid, but he still liked to verbally jab his father from time to time. It was a little game they played back and forth while fishing.

The planer board finally bobbed back up to the surface and eventually was reeled over the transom; the younger man quickly removing it from the trolling line. "There . . . ," he said. "Now it's just you and the fish, Dad. Don't horse this one. Take your time."

"You just be ready with that net," the old man growled. "And if this is a walleye and not a sheephead, you better not knock it off!"

By this time the female walleye was about played out. Her strength nearly gone, she resigned herself to being pulled along by the sharp object in the corner of her mouth. But being drawn nearer the boat, the sound of the idling motor frightened her. Summoning all her remaining strength, she made one last dive.

"She's not coming up," said the old man. "Sign of a big walleye. Get ready with that net. . . ."

"I'm ready, Dad," the younger man said. "Just get the fish to the boat."

Within a few yards of the back of the boat now, the large walleye finally gave up. With no strength left in her body, she felt herself being pulled toward the surface.

"Holy . . . !" said the older man upon finally seeing the walleye break the surface of the water. "Quick, get a net under her, Son!"

The younger man expertly slipped the landing net under the trophy walleye, lifted her from the water, and gently laid her down on the floor of the boat. Both men stood silently in awe for several seconds, gawking at the sheer size of the fish. They then simultaneously broke into whoops and hollers, slapping each other on the back.

"Look at that fish!" said the older man. "I've been fishing this lake for half a century, and that's the biggest walleye I've ever seen, let alone caught!"

"Well, that's definitely the biggest walleye I've ever seen!" said the son. "Hold the fish up, Dad, and I'll take your picture."

Because of the walleye's extreme weight and girth, the older man struggled to get the fish out of the landing net and held up long enough for a photo. The younger man snapped the shot with the camera on his new cell phone.

"That fish is gonna look great hanging on your wall, Dad," the younger man said, beaming a wide grin. "I'm glad I was here to see you catch it."

"I'm glad you were, too, Son. I'm glad we were here together."

At that point the older man got suddenly quiet, looked at the fish, then back at his son. "Put her back," he said quietly.

"What. . . ?" the son said incredulously.

"You heard me. Take the hook out of her mouth and put her back in the water. I don't need another walleye on my wall."

The younger man couldn't believe what he was hearing.

"But, Dad, are you sure. . . ?" he asked.

He knew his father was serious, so he eventually did as he was told. Taking a pair of needle-nose pliers from a tackle box, he freed the treble hook from the fish's jaw, then gently lifted her from the boat's deck.

"You sure about this, Dad?" he asked one last time, holding the fish over the water and giving his father one final chance to change his mind. "At your age, you may never catch a bigger one."

"Yes, I'm sure," the older man said. "Put her back. . . ."

The son gently slipped the huge walleye into the water, holding her tail briefly until she righted herself just below the surface. Feeling her slowly regaining strength, the son waited until the fish began struggling to free herself, then released his grip. Sensing she was at last free, the danger now past, the walleye slowly swam out of sight, disappearing back into the dark depths of Lake Erie. Would some other angler eventually catch her and end her life, or would she eventually die of old age?

• • •

What's a truly trophy-sized walleye? A 10-pounder? A 12-pounder? Even larger? A true trophy walleye is what *you* decide it is. In other words, it's your personal best fish, whether that be two pounds or 12.

My point in telling this fictional story is that no one should dictate to you what a trophy walleye is or is not. And there comes a time in every angler's life—or there should come a time—when you eventually realize that fishing is not only about catching fish. It's about the fishing itself, the doing, and spending time on the water with people you love, family and friends. And just like the older gentleman in my story, if you fish long enough you'll come to eventually realize that not every trophy fish you catch has to be killed.

Don't get me wrong. I love eating walleyes, and few of the smaller, legal-sized fish I catch are released. But I believe a large walleye is a fish that deserves added respect. If you want to take one or two to the taxidermist and hang them on your wall, fine. But how many is too many? Only you can answer that question. It's just something to think about as we end this book together.

That said, I hope to see you on the water soon. And if I can ever help you with your walleye trolling, don't hesitate to contact me. My contact information is below.

Wishing you tight lines and safe fishing. . . .

W. H. "Chip" Gross
Mailing address: 6108 Township Road 88, Fredericktown, Ohio 43019
Email: whchipgross@gmail.com
Web site: www.chipgross.com

Preparing Walleyes for the Table

The white, flaky, mild meat of walleyes makes great table fare, and keeping that excellent taste in the fish's flesh begins while you're still on the water. For instance, if you plan to keep a walleye to eat, place the fish in your boat's livewell or on ice in a cooler immediately after catching it. Taking a few photos of the fish first is certainly okay—in fact, fresh-caught walleyes make for the best photos—but as soon as you're done smiling for the camera, make sure you handle the fish appropriately.

On the Water

When I catch a walleye, while the fish is still in the landing net, the first thing I do is grab it by its lower jaw using a fish gripper. (Remember, don't stick your thumb in a walleye's mouth as you would a bass, these critters have teeth!) The fish gripper gives you control of the fish. While holding the walleye with one hand, using the gripper, I then work the hooks out of the fish's mouth with a pair of pliers.

Once the hooks are out and the fish is clear of the net, I hold the walleye over the livewell in my boat. I prefer to "bleed" walleyes, and here is how it's done. While still holding the fish by its lower jaw using the gripper, I turn the fish upside down (belly up) and slit its throat. This can be done using a small filet knife, but using a pair of game shears or heavy-duty scissors is safer—you're less likely to cut yourself. Once you've made the cut, quickly drop the walleye into the livewell and close the lid. The fish will bleed profusely as it swims in the livewell and die within a few minutes.

The reason for "bleeding" walleyes is that most if not all the blood will flow out of the fish as it dies, resulting in pearly white filets and improved taste. And less blood makes cleaning less messy, too. Obviously, you would not want to slit the throat of a trophy fish in such a way, a walleye you planned to take to a taxidermist and have mounted.

Preparations for a great tasting walleye dinner begin while you're still on the water.

An alternative to killing a trophy-sized walleye is releasing it and having a plastic replica made of the catch instead. A skilled taxidermist can produce a replica that will look amazingly like the real thing, yet endure far longer than the actual fish mount itself would. All you need do is take a few quick measurements (length and girth) and photograph the fish, then provide this information to your taxidermist.

At the end of my fishing day, I drain the water from my boat's livewell upon reaching shore and cover the walleyes with crushed ice for the ride home. If it's early spring or late fall and the water is cold, I may leave the chilly water in the livewell and forgo the ice. But if there is any question as to whether or not the walleyes could soften and spoil before I have a chance to clean them, I cover them with ice. Don't take a chance on losing your fish—and some great eating—after you've worked so hard to catch them.

Cleaning Walleyes

No one really enjoys cleaning fish, but the only thing worse than having to clean fish after a long day on the water is not cleaning fish—

meaning you didn't catch anything worth keeping. So with that philosophy in mind, here are a few tips for making the chore go more quickly and easily.

Because of their body shape, walleyes are custom made for cleaning with an electric filet knife, and if you aren't using one you're missing a time-saving bet. Laying the walleye on its side, hold it by the head with your free hand and make the first cut diagonally behind the head, just behind the gill cover. Once you feel the blades of the filet knife touch the fish's backbone, turn the knife on its side and cut all the way down the length of the fish to the tail, but not through the tail. Next, turn the filet over and, working off the edge of the cleaning table, run the knife between the skin and the filet, removing the skin and its attached scales.

You now have a filet, but it is not yet boneless, as the rib cage is still attached. At this point, I lay aside the electric knife and pick up a regular filet knife, using it to cut out the rib cage. Once that's accomplished, you have a boneless walleye filet, ready to be baked, broiled, or deep fried. Use the same procedure on the other side of the fish.

Cleaning walleyes using this method takes only a minute or two per fish once you become proficient. And two people working together, one using an electric filet knife and the other a regular filet knife, can clean walleyes very rapidly. Another tip is to keep a stainless steel bowl nearby, half-filled with ice water, in which to place the filets, keeping them chilled and firm.

Additional Materials

Since you're reading this book you're probably already an experienced angler who knows the basics of fish care and cleaning. But if not—and who couldn't learn a new tip or two now and then?—there are many media resources available that can help.

Every state wildlife agency in the United States offers free publications (both in print and online) explaining fish handling and cleaning, and most are free of charge. For free online video demonstrations on how to clean walleyes and other fish, YouTube (www.youtube.com) is a great source of information; just type "fish fileting" in the search box. Many of these online videos may not be professionally done, but you'll get the idea and the price is certainly right. For an excellent professional-quality DVD on how to clean fish, I'd suggest *Caring for the Catch* produced by In-Fisherman publications (www.in-fisherman.com).

If you don't plan to cook and eat your walleyes while still fresh, freezing is the next best alternative. Buy heavyweight plastic freezer bags, write "walleyes" on them for easy identification, and also include the date the fish were caught. Fill about half of each bag with filets and the rest of the bag with water. Seal the bag and place in a freezer. The water will surround the filets as it turns to ice, preventing freezer burn. If prepared and frozen in this manner, walleye filets will last for months in a freezer, if not years. And if you thaw the filets in the refrigerator when you're ready to eat them, rather than at room temperature, they'll taste more like fresh fish, too.

Chip's Favorite Walleye Recipe

Ingredients:

Cooking spray
¼ cup butter
2–3 cloves of garlic, finely chopped
1–2 tsp. lemon juice
2½ pounds of walleye filets
Salt and pepper
¾ cup grated Romano cheese
1 cup fine bread crumbs or cracker crumbs
Diagonally cut green onion tops or chives (optional)

Preparation:

Spray a 15 × 10-inch baking pan with cooking spray.
Melt butter. Stir in garlic and lemon.
Place walleye filets in a single layer in baking pan. Brush with butter mixture, then season with salt and pepper.
Sprinkle with Romano cheese and bread crumbs. Drizzle with remaining butter.*
Bake at 450 degrees for 10 to 12 minutes or until done.
Sprinkle with chives, if desired.

*When my wife, Jan, makes this dish, she first dips the walleye filets in the butter, then rolls them in the bread crumbs, and finally sprinkles them with the cheese, drizzling any remaining butter over the cheese-covered fish. In our oven, she cooks the filets at 475 degrees for 15 minutes, and the walleyes come out golden brown.

Hope you're hungry!

Contact Information Page

Below are the professional fishing guides, charter captains, walleye pros, and other great anglers interviewed for this book, listed alphabetically. If you have specific walleye trolling questions (or would like to book a fishing trip with them), any of these experts are more than willing to be contacted for in-depth answers. Thanks, again, to all of them for sharing their fishing secrets in *Trolling Big-Water Walleyes.*

Den Braun (tel: 440–967–3657)
Mark Brumbaugh (website: www.markbrumbaugh.com)
Joe Cinelli (website: www.niagarafishingguides.com)
Russ Clark (website: www.fishseahawk.com)
Mark Courts (website: www.onthewaterlive.com)
John Gillman (email: jgillman@atsprinting.com)
Bob Hanmer (website: www.lorainportauthority.com/links)
Keith Kavajecz (website: www.thenextbite.com)
Larry Lambert (website: www.blue777walleyecharters.com)
Mark Martin (website: www.markmartins.net)
Rich Mealey (email: orc_rich@yahoo.com)
Aaron Mcquoid (website: www.mcquoidguides.com)
Ernie Olson (tel: 320–267–9844)
Mark Romanack (website: www.fishing411.net)
Dave Rose (website: www.wildfishing.com)
Scott Stecher (website: www.reefrunner.com)
Peg Van Vleet (website: www.blueskycharters.net)
Walleye Central (website: www.walleyecentral.com)

Index